W9-BGV-385

COUNSELING WITH THE MIND OF CHRIST

The Dynamics of Spirituotherapy®

Charles R. Solomon, Ed.D.

Fleming H. Revell Company
Old Tappan, New Jersey

Unless otherwise identified, all Scripture quotations are from the King James Version of the Bible

Scripture quotations identified NIV are from the NEW INTERNATIONAL VERSION. Copyright © 1973 by New York International Bible Society. Used by permission.

Diagram #5 (Wheel) and Diagram #6 (Line) first appeared in *Handbook to Happiness* by Charles R. Solomon, published by Tyndale House Publishers.

Library of Congress Cataloging in Publication Data

Solomon, Charles R.
    Counseling with the mind of Christ.

    Bibliography: p.
    1. Pastoral counseling. 2. Counseling. I. Title.
BV4012.2.S64   253.5   77-12227
ISBN 0-8007-5049-7

Copyright © 1977 by Charles R. Solomon
Published by Fleming H. Revell Company
All rights reserved
Printed in the United States of America

TO all those who have shared their lives with me in the counseling office I am deeply indebted. My life has been immeasurably enriched by their love, friendship, and spiritual insights. As we have hurt together and learned together, it is my earnest desire that this product of those experiences may be a tool for them and others to learn more effectively to "bear . . . one another's burdens" (Galatians 6:2) and to ". . . comfort them which are in any trouble, by the comfort wherewith we ourselves are comforted of God" (2 Corinthians 1:4).

Acknowledgments

I owe a debt of gratitude for typing and retyping of the manuscript to my wife, Sue; to my daughters Cathy and Susan; to Verna Griggs; and to Loretta Naslund for final typing. Also, a thank-you goes to Helen Hudson and Mike Baty for reading the manuscript and for their suggestions.

Acknowledgments

Contents

Life: Riddle or Reason

Is life becoming too much to bear—
Are you weary and sore distressed?
Have you searched in vain for peace of mind—
A place of belonging and rest?
Have you considered the meaning of life
In a senseless, troubled world?
Does it seem, alas, that fate is unfair
In the things at you it has hurled?

Are you ever tempted to despair
In the world's mad rush for pleasure?
Do you see the folly of the fruitless search
For happiness based on Earth's treasure?
As you answer *yes* to the queries above
You join an ever-increasing throng,
Who have tried all the world has to offer
And are dismayed to find they've been wrong.

But all is not lost if you're willing
To disdain the offerings of Earth
And look instead to its Maker   (*Heb. 12:2*)
And see things of eternal worth.
God has spoken to us through the Bible   (*1 John 5:11*)
And through Jesus, His only Son,   (*Heb. 1:2*)
We have but to heed His message
And the victory for us He has won.   (*2 Cor. 2:14*)

Our sins were taken to Calvary
As the blessed Lord Jesus there died;   (*1 Pet. 2:24*)
We have in Him a sure refuge
In which we are bidden to hide.   (*Col. 3:3*)
God's love is abundantly shown us   (*Rom. 5:8*)
As on Jesus His fury was spent;
A new life He surely secured us
As from the Mount to heav'n He went.   (*Acts 1:9*)

The sins of a lifetime are forgiven
As we to God do confess: (*1 John 1:9*)
When we trust Jesus as Lord and Savior   (*Rom. 10:9, 10*)
With life eternal He does bless.   (*Rom. 6:23*)
Not only were sins borne at Calvary   (*Rom. 5:8*)
But our old selves were taken there, too;   (*Rom. 6:6*)
With Him in death, old things pass away   (*2 Cor. 5:17*)
And all things in Him are made new.

When things of the world are viewed from above,   (*Eph. 2:6*)
The end from the beginning is seen;
As in Jesus we learn to abide,   (*John 15:4, 5, 7*)
Our lives, too, become quite serene.
The troubled waters He commands to still   (*Matt. 8:26*)
And in green pastures bids us lie;   (*Ps. 23:2*)
The world in turmoil does remain,   (*John 16:33*)
And with His peace cannot vie.   (*John 14:27*)

I bid you come to Him today   (*2 Cor. 5:20*)
And be freed from all your sin;
Your death on Calvary He did die   (*2 Cor. 5:14*)
That you a new life could begin.
Turn to Him without delay
And find that sought-for rest;   (*Matt. 11:28–30*)
Turmoil and pain will pass away
As in Him you are blessed.

Then your life in Christ is hidden in God   (*Col. 3:3*)
And all spiritual blessings you gain;   (*Eph. 1:3*)
The things of this world lose their pull
And only things eternal remain.
Together we look for the blessed hope—   (*Titus 2:12, 13*)
And eagerly await that loud cry;   (*1 Thess. 4:16*)
His coming back will be as He went,   (*Acts 1:11*)
And we will meet Him in the sky!   (*1 Thess. 4:17*)

Amen. Even so, come, Lord Jesus.   (*Rev. 22:20*)

Introduction

A word of explanation is in order for the person who is unfamiliar with the counseling ministry of Grace Fellowship International (GFI) and who has not read the author's first two books, *Handbook to Happiness* and *The Ins and Out of Rejection*. It is necessary that the reader understand, experientially, his identification with Christ in death, burial, resurrection, ascension, and seating at the right hand of God in heaven if he is to derive the desired benefit from the book. Those who are not accustomed to the term *identification* may prefer such synonyms as the "abundant life," "victorious life," "lordship," "Spirit-filled or Spirit-controlled life," or the normal Christian life of Watchman Nee.

The underlying spiritual message is that of understanding and appropriating by faith the resources to be found in Christ through the believer's union with Him. Though all who have been born into Christ (John 3:3) are *united* to Him and are heirs to all that He *is* (Romans 8:16, 17), comparatively few have come to the end of their own resources and have begun to live the life that is Christ, or to live on His resources. This being the case, the many who have come to the end of their resources must turn to resources outside themselves. Ours has become a credit-card economy, so that those who have exhausted their financial resources can borrow or sponge off the resources of others. In like manner, those who have seemingly exhausted their resources in their spouses may turn to an affair to satisfy a craving for emotional support, fleshly lust, prestige, acceptance, or escape.

In a society where it is not only condoned but encouraged to the point of near brainwashing to live beyond your means or

11

resources, nothing could be more natural than to turn to the world system in an attempt to live beyond emotional resources as well. When liaisons with other people fail to meet such needs, the "credit card" of ingested drugs such as alcohol, tranquilizers, and the like is used to live beyond emotional or psychic resources. Just as in fiscal indebtedness, the piper must eventually be paid. Barring some windfall, it is usually necessary to repay when fiscal supplies are yet flagging, with the additional burden of interest! When the person comes to the point where he is emotionally bankrupt and the drugs no longer suffice, therapy is a generally accepted means of bootstrapping to propel the human vehicle as far as *humanly* possible, though some procedures such as electroshock may approach being inhuman.

It is in just such a dilemma that a person is most open to an answer outside himself, because he has tried everything he knows and has yet to find a satisfying answer. It is a sad commentary on Christianity that many Christians go the worldly credit-card route oblivious of the fact that the indwelling Spirit is incomparably superior to ingested drugs or imposed therapy. The emotional and mental damage sustained through traumatic experiences and adverse circumstances condition the individual to react to persons and life in a negative manner; and, in turn, they are usually responded to in kind. When the internal pain is intolerable and no answer is evident, many, or even most, turn to fleeting thoughts of death as the only escape from the impossible situation. If not presented with a viable alternative, some pursue these thoughts to their consummation in suicide. This process is lucidly portrayed in a recent book by John Stevens (with a Foreword by Solomon), *Suicide—An Illicit Lover* (Heritage House). In his book as in *the* Book, the Bible, the one and only answer is given—a type of death which issues in Life, crucifixion with Christ:

"I am [have been] crucified with Christ: nevertheless I live; yet not I, but Christ liveth in me: and the life which I now live in the flesh I live by the faith of the Son of God, who loved me, and gave himself for me" (Galatians 2:20).

It is this "life out of death" principle which is delineated in the author's first book, *Handbook to Happiness* (Tyndale) and further clarified in the second, *The Ins and Out of Rejection* (Heritage House).

It is not to be inferred that mastering the contents of this book will result in the development of a qualified counselor. However, under the tutelage of the Holy Spirit, the reader may begin to learn to share with others from the Word of God in a manner which will enjoy His blessing.

Those who would become effective counselors in a vocational setting should avail themselves of training consistent with the location in which they intend to work. The term *Spirituotherapy* is a registered trade mark of Grace Fellowship International to identify materials, and its use is not permitted by those utilizing such materials in advertising their services. The reason for this is that GFI cannot assure those receiving such counseling that the counselor does not deviate from the approach outlined in the materials published under its auspices.

Those desiring training either at the lay or professional level should contact Grace Fellowship International, 200 South Sheridan, Denver, Colorado 80226. Short-term and extended training is available at the Denver location; staff members are available for conferences and lectures at remote locations.

Although male pronouns are used throughout this book for ease of expression, it is not to be inferred that the male gender is responsible for all the problems—nor that it is endowed with all the answers!

1

The Christian As Counselor

Our Heritage

During the last two decades there have been several approaches to Christian counseling or Christian psychology proffered as scriptural methods of integrating the disciplines of theology and psychology. This rapprochement was effected after years of hostility when psychiatry was openly rejected by ministers who tenaciously held to the Word of God and psychology was held suspect by a great many men of the cloth. As in so many controversial issues, there has been a swinging of the pendulum to the opposite extreme; and the Christian with graduate training in the behavioral sciences is accorded a power which eclipses that claimed or manifested by the man called of God to minister the Word in the power of the Spirit.

Therapists, of all people, are the first to admit that they are not the panacea in dealing with the personal problems faced by all of us in the seventies. They, too, are divided as to the approach to be used and results to be expected in psychotherapy with those experiencing mental and emotional disturbances. New and used approaches are being utilized with varying degrees of effectiveness, along with combinations and variations cropping up with unsettling regularity. All too frequently, the minister ascribes more power to the therapist than he, himself, claims. The therapist is painfully aware of the woeful inadequacy of every approach to psychotherapy as recorded in the annals of research. Even so, the minister knows that the training he received in the typical Bible college or seminary does not render him capable of even tackling the problems with which the therapist grapples —much less seeing greater results.

Direct and indirect support of the disciplines of psychology and psychiatry by the Christian community is a tacit admission that the Word of God and the Spirit of God are insufficient resources to meet the deepest needs of man. The indictment here is not of the psychologist or the psychiatrist but rather, of the institutions of theological training which have deferred to the developments of the world system and thereby turned out generations of ministers with an inferiority complex. Rare, indeed, is the minister who routinely counsels with and sees God release those who suffer from that indefinable malady termed "mental illness." This is not to say that psychology has nothing to offer in understanding human conflict, but that the psychological principles should not be used as a prescribing tool.

A nationally known theologian has made the assertion that the psychologist and psychiatrist have done more harm to the cause of fundamental Christianity than all of the liberal theologians combined. The liberal theologian has been recognized for his "contribution" in undermining the Word of God, but the humanistic developments in the field of psychotherapy are much more subtle in their encroachment upon scriptural answers to human needs. It is even *more* difficult to ferret out when the humanistic answer is couched in or surrounded by quotations from Scripture. Or, to go a step further, assiduous application of scriptural principles to human behavior on the part of the therapist and client alike may yet be done in the energy of the flesh. Since the average Christian has flesh or self in the ascendancy, it is difficult, if not impossible, for him to discern that scriptural principles for human behavior applied by the flesh remain flesh. Indeed 1 Corinthians 2:10–16 makes it abundantly clear that such things are spiritually discerned. The natural mind cannot discern such things, and neither can the unrenewed mind (Romans 12:2) of the Christian.

Several years of counseling and working with ministers and

missionaries have revealed that the average minister has not appropriated Christ as his life, which means that he is walking after the flesh. Though this assertion is not based on statistical data, it has been confirmed by one minister after another as he has understood the precious truth of his union with Christ in His death and resurrection life. It stands to reason that a smaller percentage of therapists would have such understanding than those trained for the gospel ministry. This being the case, the average Christian who is practicing psychology or psychiatry must lean heavily on the humanistic science which he studied in the secular environment. As a born-again believer, he may lead his clients to Christ and inculcate scriptural principles of learning and behavior, and yet be unaware that a fleshly tool has usurped and supplanted the deeper therapy of the Holy Spirit as pertains to emotional and mental needs—his own and those of his clients.

The foregoing will serve to alert the reader that educators in the Christian community have all but abdicated in past years in deference to Christian psychologists and psychiatrists, when faced with training ministerial students so they will have the proficiency required to adequately prepare them for counseling with those in mental and emotional distress. To be sure, there are those who are unable to care for themselves, or who are dangerous to themselves or others who must have custodial care. Though Christ is the answer for such persons, the typical pastor or Christian counselor cannot provide facilities to care for these needs while supplying the spiritual counsel. Unless and until such facilities are available, there is no choice but to refer the person for hospitalization. In all cases where there is indication of physiological malfunction, the counselor should work closely with a sympathetic physician; here, too, it is difficult to find a Christian physician who is not allied with the humanistic approaches to mental and emotional symptoms.

The seventies have seen a resurgence of approaches to counseling based on the Word of God. This will become increasingly the case as the world situation continues to darken and the various approaches to therapy are forcibly stripped of their veneer, revealing their lack of foundation in truth. Given a situation where only committed Christians who can transcend this world system are able to stand, the best of therapists are bound to fall as their foundations crumble.

Christian Counseling

Having briefly assessed the world system offerings, and as amended by integration with Scriptures and scriptural principles, more or less, let's turn to the Christian counseling scene.

Christian counseling has never enjoyed the reputation for results it should have had because, in the main, it has also leaned heavily on the arm of the flesh. "Christian counseling," therefore, can mean anything or nothing. There are those who employ the term, and advertise themselves as practicing such to avoid the licensing required to do psychotherapy—who may be ineffective in their counseling as well as dishonest in their representation of themselves and their services. At the other extreme are those who employ Scripture to such an extent that adequate psychological understanding of the genesis and nature of the symptoms is not provided the individual. In the middle is that group which waters down the Word of God and psychotherapy to the detriment of both! *Rare, indeed, is the individual who employs psychology exclusively for purposes of understanding the psychodynamics of the behavior in question while allowing the Spirit of God to apply the Word of God to produce a child of God and that child being "conformed to His image"* (*see* Romans 8:29).

The flesh being what it is, the Christian community has all but embraced the idea that extensive graduate education is an absolute must, if one is to be effective in being of help to a disturbed individual. Having been perpetrated by the world system, this deception has been nurtured by schools of theological education which teach ministerial students to "refer" when it is appropriat. at they *defer* to the Word of God and the power of the Holy Spirit. As previously stated, there are extreme cases which should be referred but these are a small minority. When ministers are educated to refer or *defer* to the world system on a mass basis, it is little wonder that the average Joe Blow layman would deem himself totally inadequate to be of help to disturbed persons. Indeed, the minister, when in need of help for himself or his family, is "faked out" by believing that it is emotional/mental illness and is referred or self-referred outside the church for a substitute answer.

A case in point is a minister whose wife was supposedly having a nervous breakdown and was told by a physician to seek psychiatric help immediately. She was suffering from internal tremors which prevented relaxation, sleep, and so forth. Her husband, meanwhile, had been somewhat successful in masking depression just as deep as hers. Privately, he would have welcomed a "reason" to leave the ministry which would have permitted him to save face. He knew he needed help but was reluctant to get it, because of the social stigma and threat to his professional competency. He was unable to divulge this to his wife for fear it would cause her to go under completely! As he called for an appointment for his wife, he was very skeptical of a spiritual approach to her problem. Upon initiation of counseling, he freely admitted that he needed help as badly as did his wife; however, he had not been taught in a fundamental seminary that such symptoms dating back to childhood in their genesis would ever respond to spiritual counseling. By the end of an afternoon of counseling, both minister and wife had appropriated Christ as life as they received Spirit-given insight into both the symptoms and the answer. After two more hours the next morning, they went back to their church to share with their people what the Holy Spirit had done to the glory of God! Is it surprising, then, that the lay people in that fundamental church did not have access to the answer to similar needs in their own lives? To take it a step further, it is very easy to see how the *intra*personal problems in a church could result in sufficient *inter*personal problems that a person or group of persons being separated from the church could be quite a common occurrence!

Not only should the minister who is called of God to minister the life of Christ be able to help disturbed individuals, but also, the rank-and-file Christian should be able to do likewise. The word *counselor* in itself is sufficient to deter most Christians from holding themselves out as persons who have the answers for those in need. The average Christian today would emphatically deny that he is a counselor and would probably thwart all attempts to make him one. There are several reasons why this is so, but a faulty understanding of the meaning of the term and a lack of training and/or understanding of Christian growth and witness, would encompass most of them.

The average person thinks of a counselor as a problem-solver who gives advice on a wide range of difficult situations and who has extensive formal training in psychology and counseling techniques. This would be an apt description of most of those persons currently in the counseling field, and an understanding of psychology and methods of relating to people can be an asset or a liability for an individual who would be a "helping person," depending upon its use. Since there has been a breakdown in communicating to those who know Christ—how He can provide the resources to meet their needs—they have not been equipped to communicate it to others. Thus, the help or comfort which could be given to others (2 Corinthians 1:3, 4) has been effectively blocked and this role has been assumed by the professional. All too frequently, this professional is not the minister but someone outside the confines of the Church. The psychologists, psychiatrists, and professional counselors have taken on a role in working with intrapersonal and interpersonal problems which, in times past, were the domain of the church.

The first-century Church knew nothing of such professionals in coping with mental and emotional difficulties which, no doubt, existed at that time. There have been Christians down through history who have been prepared by the Holy Spirit to act as spiritual guides for those who were in dire need. One has only to read of Madame Guyon and Fénelon, among others, who in the seventeenth century were effectively used of God in this manner. Christianity, in the main, is so shallow that we refer to such persons as "mystics" and thereby excuse ourselves from performing such functions in the Body of Christ today.

Christ-centered Counseling

Having dispensed with some of the things that Christian counseling isn't, let's proceed to what it should be. Stated simply, it is leading another person in understanding and appropriating all that the Lord Jesus Christ is for all that he needs, both here and hereafter. "To them God has chosen to make known among the Gentiles the glorious riches of this mystery, which is Christ in you, the hope of Glory. We proclaim him, *counseling and teaching everyone with all wisdom,* so that we may present everyone perfect in Christ . . ." (Colossians 1:27, 28 NIV, *italics added*). The object of the counseling and teaching in the foregoing passage is to bring those with whom we deal to maturity in Christ. Such counseling endeavors, first of all, to lead a person to trust the Lord Jesus Christ as Savior and Lord and then to disciple him in spiritual growth. As will be discovered later in the book, a person is met where he is and helped to understand his psychological and/or interpersonal difficulties; but the focus is on the manner in which the life can be transformed by the renewing of the mind (Romans 12:2) through the work of the Holy Spirit, making the life of Christ a viable reality within the believer.

To become very simplistic (a term which is sometimes used to describe this approach to counseling in a derogatory manner), Christ-centered counseling could be defined as witnessing. The counselor, or Christian, is merely describing to another how the Lord Jesus Christ has transformed his own life and how that person may experience the same transformation. It *is* simple because the *gospel* is simple; if it were so complicated as to require graduate degrees to understand it, God would have passed over the great preponderance of people.

In witnessing to unsaved persons, care should be taken to

avoid lengthy dealing with symptoms such as references to "the heathen," "hypocrites in the Church," and so forth. In witnessing to Christians the same is true; it is good to understand the mental and emotional symptoms and the living problems, but the counselor or witness must avoid becoming embroiled in them. The goal in witnessing to the unsaved is to lead them to Christ; the goal in witnessing to Christians is to lead them to the Cross. There are many parallels which may be drawn between the two types of witnessing.

Not all Christians are called to be counselors, but *all are commanded to be witnesses* (Acts 1:8). We are to be witnesses not only to His power to save our immortal souls but also to His grace and power to . . . "supply all your need according to his riches in glory by Christ Jesus" (Philippians 4:19). May God grant that you will not be content with playing around at the shore and that He will thrust you out into the deeps where He alone can sustain you. Having learned that invaluable lesson, you will undoubtedly be a source of sustenance and guidance to others, as you teach them to feed on Him and to walk in the Spirit (Galatians 5:16).

2

Counselor Preparation

God is very specific in the training He gives for the work He calls us to do. His training program is not identical for any two counselors. The primary source of preparation is that hammered out in living through the necessa_y experiences that force one to the Word to glean the food essential to spiritual growth. The assignment He is going to give has much to do with the type and extent of training required. Since Christ-centered counseling has been defined heretofore as a specialized approach to *witnessing,* it makes a difference for training purposes whether the person will be involved in vocational Christian service or in a lay capacity. All Christians are expected to be evangelists but not all by vocation. Similarly, all Christians should be able to witness to others about the power of the Cross in the life of the believer, but not all are called to do this as a vocation.

The person whom God calls to vocational Christian counseling of this nature has generally suffered considerable emotional and mental anguish. Since the Cross entails suffering and he will be constantly dealing with those in the midst of turmoil, the cauldron of suffering (Isaiah 48:10) is his best "boot camp." Instruction is vital, but putting it into practice where the tire meets the road is the acid test of reality.

For the purposes of this writing, it will be assumed that the counselor in question is of the full-time variety. The preparation for such will be considered under three headings: spiritual, practical, and calling.

Spiritual Preparation

Spiritual maturity is the sine qua non in the making of the spiritual counselor.

Although the symptoms will be as varied as those counseled, the ultimate goal is aiding and guiding the person in spiritual growth. In bringing a person to maturity in Christ, the Holy Spirit must engineer the demise of the self-life through the Cross. To work in close cooperation with the Spirit, the counselor must first have gone over the road to the Cross and have appropriated the work of the Cross in his own life. Also, he must have successfully negotiated the terrain beyond the Cross if he is to know firsthand the perils of the victorious life and the spiritual warfare it necessarily entails.

As he travels the road to spiritual maturity, the instructions and warnings are to be gained from the Word of God. He may have experiences and learn from experience, but his primary source of learning is to be from the Word under the tutelage of the Holy Spirit, with all "experiences" to be tried and tested by the Word, rather than used in attempts to force the Word to conform to or confirm experience. As the believer learns and grows he finds that he cannot force others into his mold and conform them to his experience. To be sure, there are commonalities which may be used as general criteria in evaluating spiritual growth, but there is great diversity within commonality.

The counselor who does not hold to the inerrancy of the Scriptures does not have a sure foundation on which to build. He must have absolute faith in the Word of God and in the God of the Word if he is to be able to communicate implicit trust to those to whom he would minister. He must believe in a God of miracles if he expects to do counseling and see lives change without his resorting to therapy; the only way to really believe in miracles is to have witnessed and experienced them. Any time we see God intervene in the affairs of men, we say it is miraculous; but, to God, it is just business as usual!

The counselor's success in his experience with men will be in direct proportion to his success in his experience with God. His must be a Cross-centered theology and a Christ-centered life; if he stays at the Cross he has a message of death—the view from the heavenlies is of resurrection life. He must have appropriated the Cross in his own life along with intellectual understanding if he is to understand how to lead others there. He must walk with the Lord if he is to teach others how to walk in the Spirit.

In sum, the spiritual preparation consists of a life where self has been dealt a deathblow and the person has sufficient experience on the resurrection side of the Cross to minister the Christ-life in the power of the Spirit through the skilled use of the Word.

Practical Preparation

The type and extent of training for Christ-centered counseling depends largely upon the setting in which the counseling is to be done and the clientele involved. Generally speaking, Bible-school education is highly recommended and, in some settings, might be required. Seminary training could be an asset or a liability, depending upon the emphasis of the institution. Similarly, formal training in psychology can be very helpful, if kept in proper perspective with Scripture. Almost without exception, those who receive graduate education in psychology are trained in some form of psychotherapy. It is one thing to use psychology for purposes of understanding past and present behavior; it is yet another to do therapy which serves to strengthen and patch up the flesh or self.

Though formal training in theology and psychology is not decried, the state of the art in Christ-centered counseling has not advanced to the place where the two have been wedded at the Cross in formal degree programs except in specialized cases. At this writing there are a few colleges where this approach to counseling is beginning to find favor, though minimal instruction is available.

In the meantime, it is necessary to secure the practical training through home study, conferences, workshops, etc. GFI continues to expand such training opportunities, as the Lord leads, in short-term training with longer periods of training available on a selective basis. Training through additional media will also be available as God supplies funds and personnel to produce the materials. The goal of such training is to teach a person who has appropriated Christ as life to communicate the identification truths to another in such a way that he, too, might enter into victory by faith. Formal education is not mandatory and could actually prejudice the learner against the simplicity that is in Christ Jesus (2 Corinthians 11:3). When man in his sophistry develops techniques to supplant the work intended to be done by the Holy Spirit, it is certain to be complicated. Once mastered, it is difficult for most to lay it aside in deference to God's method.

The practical training to be used of the Lord in this way is really old-fashioned discipleship taught by the Holy Spirit using persons skilled in the Word of God. Those who have been involved in witnessing to unbelievers will find the ground rules to be the same. The message is still Christ; the method remains by grace through faith. The sinner must understand the power of the Blood to forgive sins; the Christian must understand the power of the Cross to deal with the flesh.

Calling

As in any ministry, a person who would assay to enter full-time counseling must be assured of God's leading. If God has truly called one to such a ministry in a particular place and the timing is right, God will supply the needs and bless him and the ministry with miraculous results. If a person merely learns a technique and makes a decision to enter the field because he has the proper education, God is under no such obligation and the enterprise is doomed to mediocrity or failure.

A person should demonstrate God's utilization of his life in the manner herein described in a lay capacity before considering doing such counseling on a professional basis. When this is done, other spiritual persons will be able to attest to God's leading in his life. Such persons would qualify for training and would very quickly be of great service to the Body of Christ in ministering to those who are hampered in spiritual growth and ministry by mental and emotional symptoms or by other difficulties hampering their personal and interpersonal affairs.

3

A Simplified Model of Man

In considering the makeup of man, we must consider him in his estranged relationship to God as well as exploring the riches in glory available to the Christian. To do this, we look at what he was *in Adam* as contrasted with what he is *in Christ*. The first diagram describes our overall position *in Adam* and *in Christ,* with subsequent diagrams depicting the conditions which obtain *within* the individual's makeup considering his relationship to God or lack of it.

Diagram 1 depicts the chasm which exists between our inheritance in Adam and our inheritance in Christ. The Cross is shown as the one and only bridge which will span the gulf by cutting off what we were in Adam through death while bringing into existence a new dimension, *resurrection life.* First Corinthians 15:22 states it succinctly: "For as in Adam all die, even so in Christ shall all be made alive." Since Adam is the federal head of the human race, his sin and his death through sin constituted all of his progeny sinners. Since all were born in vital union with Adam's nature, it follows that all were partakers of that nature.

The Lord Jesus Christ was also the federal head of a new race: "And so it is written, The first man Adam was made a living soul; the last Adam was made a quickening [life-giving] spirit" (1 Corinthians 15:45). In other words the first man, Adam, was made a living soul by having the Spirit breathed in; and he became a *dying* soul as he died spiritually in the *day* (Genesis 2:17) of his transgression. The death sentence was

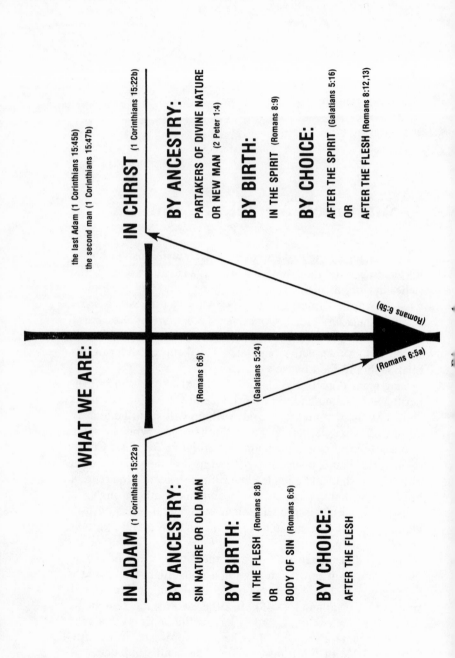

WHAT WE ARE:

IN ADAM (1 Corinthians 15:22a)

BY ANCESTRY:
SIN NATURE OR OLD MAN

BY BIRTH:
IN THE FLESH (Romans 8:8)
OR
BODY OF SIN (Romans 6:6)

BY CHOICE:
AFTER THE FLESH

the last Adam (1 Corinthians 15:45b)
the second man (1 Corinthians 15:47b)

IN CHRIST (1 Corinthians 15:22b)

BY ANCESTRY:
PARTAKERS OF DIVINE NATURE
OR NEW MAN (2 Peter 1:4)

BY BIRTH:
IN THE SPIRIT (Romans 8:9)

BY CHOICE:
AFTER THE SPIRIT (Galatians 5:16)
OR
AFTER THE FLESH (Romans 8:12,13)

(Romans 6:6)

(Galatians 5:24)

(Romans 6:5b)

(Romans 6:5a)

carried out immediately in his spirit, but he continued to function in his soul (personality) and body, albeit separated from God.

The Lord Jesus Christ as the last Adam was made to be sin that He might represent us in death (2 Corinthians 5:14, 15), and in victory over sin and death, through resurrection. "Therefore if any man be in Christ, he is a new creature; old things are passed away [at the cross]; behold, all things are become new [in resurrection life]" (2 Corinthians 5:17). By one man came death; by Another came life—eternal life.

Diagram 1 places into perspective position and practice in relationship to the Cross. Looking first at our position *in Adam,* we find that as descendants of fallen man we were made partakers of his sin nature (Romans 5:12), which is also known as our *"old* man." Other appellations for this spiritual nature are: *Adamic nature, dead spirit, old nature,* and *old sin nature.* By contrast, we were made partakers of the divine nature (2 Peter 1:4) by virtue of our new birth when we received the life of Christ (1 John 5:11, 12). Or, as Ephesians 4:22–24 states it, we have put off the "old man" and put on the "new man." This "putting off" was done by the operation of the Cross, according to Romans 6:6. Our ancestry provided us with a sin nature and constituted us as "flesh" or "in the flesh," as stated in Romans 8:8. Romans 8:9 shows us that a transition has taken place, since we are no longer "in the flesh, but in the Spirit." Since we are no longer "in the flesh," something must have happened to change our position. That word *position* should be underscored at this point, since it is not to be confused with *condition* or *practice.* The person who is in a *position* of "flesh" can do nothing other than walk or practice *after* the flesh; he has no other option unless and until he trusts the Lord Jesus Christ. Then, he is *in Christ* and "in the Spirit"— not "in the flesh."

The person who is "in Christ" may *live* as he has been *born* (or reborn) "in the Spirit" or "after the Spirit"; or he may resume a practice or condition of being "*after* the flesh," though he is no longer "*in* the flesh."

To further elucidate this truth it is necessary to go back to see how God dealt with the nature of man and follow it through into position and practice. Romans 6:6 states that the old man was crucified that the body of sin might be destroyed. Some would permit the old man or sin nature to revive at times and point it out as the source of sins in the Christian. Since the sin nature is a *spiritual* nature, this would somehow interweave it with man's regenerated spirit which is indwelt by the Holy Spirit—an impossible phenomenon! Also, a regenerated man would thus become a *four*-part being: body, soul, old nature, and new nature. If the old nature were intact and operative in the Christian, he could lose his salvation or become demon-possessed after having had a spiritual birth, depending upon which nature happened to be in ascendancy at the moment.

To return to Romans 6:6, the Holy Spirit doesn't use unnecessary words, and we have the old man crucified "that the body of sin might be destroyed." What is this "body of sin"? Many commentators would have us believe that this speaks of the physical body, while many, if not most, of the same commentators would not identify "the body of the sins of the flesh" in Colossians 2:11 as the physical body. Also, in Romans 7:24 we have a similar phrase, "the body of this death," which some of the same commentators again define as the physical body. It is the author's position that these phrases are alike in describing the *position* of "flesh"—that this "body of sin" might be defined as the *vehicle* or *carrier* of sins. The old man was crucified that the vehicle or carrier of sins might be put out of business. It is not that the position of "flesh" has been crucified per se but that the source of its power, sin operating through the old man, has been robbed of its authority to enslave through the crucifixion of the old man. Colossians 2:12, 13 makes it patently clear that the "body of the sins of the flesh" has been dealt with through the believer's union with Christ in death, burial, and resurrection.

Galatians 5:24 seems to support this thesis as it states "they that are Christ's have crucified the flesh"; this statement is all-inclusive as pertains to believers—none are exempt. Yet we know that the greater percentage of Christians operate or walk "*after* the flesh."

Thus, we conclude that the *position* or *standing* before God of being "in the flesh" no longer exists, since its patron—the old man—has been cut off through death. Contrary to popular belief, this does not support, condone, or teach the doctrine of sinless perfection; the sins committed by the Christian emanate from the *condition* of flesh—a personality dominated by the power of indwelling sin. Although the agent distributing the power (the old man) has been put out of business through death, the energy force (power of the indwelling sin) yet remains. It merely finds a new channel in the believer and works directly on and through the personality, or soul, with the permission of the will.

To summarize, the unbeliever, *in Adam,* has a *sin* nature by *ancestry,* is in the flesh by *birth,* and is after the flesh by *choice.* The believer, *in Christ,* has a *new* nature by *ancestry,* is in the Spirit by *birth* and, by *choice,* may walk *after* the Spirit or *after* the flesh; if he walks after or according to the flesh, the power of indwelling sin energizes the personality to produce sins, with inevitable conflict in the soul.

Makeup of Man

With the position on the nature of man established, we now move on to the effect that man's nature h੭s on his personality and behavior. It is not the author's purpose or intention to present a lengthy discourse to prove the validity of his position or to refute contrary positions. The purpose is to state as simply as possible the threefold nature of man as spirit, soul, and body (1 Thessalonians 5:23) and to describe the interrelationships in a functional manner. The possibility of the division of soul and spirit is further buttressed by Scripture in Hebrews 4:12. Theologically, this is known as the trichotomous position, whereas man as body and soul (with some admixture of spirit) is known as the dichotomous position.

It is of signal importance to "rightly divide" the functions of the soul and spirit, the attributes of each, and the interrelationships involved. Man's nature is depicted as the focal point of the functioning or energizing of the personality; the quality of life (or death) emanating from the spirit of man will dictate the quality of behavior, whether of life unto life or death unto death (2 Corinthians 2:16).

Since we are basing the model of man on the Scripture, we will consider man from three standpoints: the natural man (1 Corinthians 2:14), carnal (1 Corinthians 3:1) or fleshly man, and the spiritual man (1 Corinthians 3:1). The natural man is man as he is born—"dead in trespasses and sins" (Ephesians 2:1)—as depicted in Diagram 2. He is born ". . . in the flesh . . ." (Romans 8:8) and, as such, cannot please God. He is a slave to sin under the despotic control of the old man or sin nature. Diagram 2 indicates the centrality of the sin nature and man's control by it.

Man's soul, principally the mind, is the battleground for the control of his being; whatever or whoever controls his mind will control his behavior. Satan, the enemy of souls, is the author of sin and works through the corrupted spirit or sin nature to control the natural man's personality (shaded to depict the *position* of flesh or the "body of sin"). He is a slave to sin, and the result of sin in the body (also shaded) will be physical death.

It is important to note that the "dead spirit" is not inoperative but, rather, is dead toward God; it is very much alive to Satan and functions in the role of the old man or sin nature. Acts 26:18 indicates that natural man lives in darkness because of the power of Satan; his "eyes" must be opened by the Holy Spirit to "see" his spiritual condition that he might receive Christ and have a spiritual birth. Since relatively few persons are physically blind, it is safe to say that this passage refers to the understanding of the mind. Thus, the diagram shows the mind as being darkened, which effectively binds or enslaves the will. The will acts either upon knowledge from the mind or impulses from the emotions. Responsible behavior, even from a human standpoint, must be anchored in objectivity, which necessitates having facts in the mind. The emotions are to the

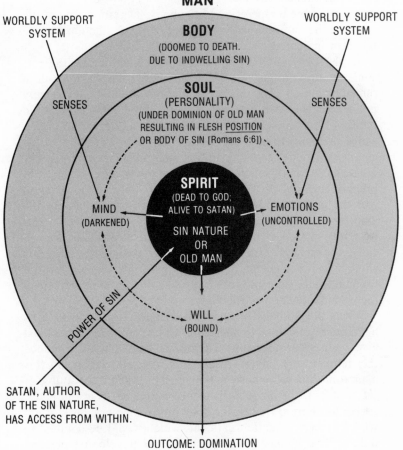

NATURAL OR UNREGENERATE MAN

WORLDLY SUPPORT SYSTEM

WORLDLY SUPPORT SYSTEM

BODY
(DOOMED TO DEATH.
DUE TO INDWELLING SIN)

SOUL
(PERSONALITY)
(UNDER DOMINION OF OLD MAN
RESULTING IN FLESH <u>POSITION</u>
OR BODY OF SIN [Romans 6:6])

SENSES

SENSES

SPIRIT
(DEAD TO GOD;
ALIVE TO SATAN)

MIND
(DARKENED)

EMOTIONS
(UNCONTROLLED)

SIN NATURE
OR
OLD MAN

POWER OF SIN

WILL
(BOUND)

SATAN, AUTHOR
OF THE SIN NATURE,
HAS ACCESS FROM WITHIN.

OUTCOME: DOMINATION

Diagram 2

soul what temperature is to the body. When the body is functioning properly the person is seldom aware that he *has* a temperature; unusual circumstances—bad or good—can result in a variation in the temperature of the body. Determination of the cause of the variation is in order that corrective action may be taken, if indicated.

Similarly, a condition in the emotions which draws the person's attention to his emotional state may or may not result in remedial action. Happiness or elation would be extremely noticeable but very pleasant, so that remedial action would hardly be considered! On the other hand, anxiety is an urgent signal that something must be done, and time is usually of the essence. An emergency condition such as impending disaster creates an anxiety situation which signals the adrenal glands to prepare for fight or flight. As the appropriate action is taken and the person perceives with his mind that all is well, the emotions eventually get the message and a degree of tranquility returns. Anxiety of the same proportions without a known cause, or anxiety from a situation with no known solution, is similar to an abnormally high temperature that cannot be brought under control; both will have a deleterious effect on the organic makeup of the body.

When the body is invaded by an alien organism such as amoeba, the elevated temperature which results may be almost a secondary consideration. Taking drastic measures to reduce the temperature might result in some alleviation of this symptom—but more basic action must be taken if the source of the problem, the amoeba, is to be eliminated from the body. Anything short of ridding the body of the alien organism or life would be symptomatic treatment, which would be doomed to failure. The human body is capable of developing defense mechanisms to cope with the continual presence of amoebic conditions, as witness people of the underdeveloped countries who live on food that tourists dare not eat.

When anxiety is treated as the problem, not as a symptomatic indicator, there may be some success in its reduction through the inauguration of defense mechanisms, but the source remains untouched. The alien life, the old man or sin nature, is not killed out in the unbeliever, but it is actually aided in its death grip upon its hapless victim. The Holy Spirit's conviction of the unbeliever will frequently result in anxiety. Such anxiety is purposeful in that it properly drives the individual to find peace through the new birth. An unbelieving therapist would neither recognize the cause of the anxiety nor be able to supply the solution.

The emotions are described in Diagram 2 as being "uncontrolled," since the state of mind being reflected has no stabilizing influence other than itself and the sin nature, which is thoroughly undependable! This being the case, the will has no other recourse than to turn to humanistic solutions—unless the choice is made to yield to Christ as Savior and Lord under the convicting and restraining influence of the Holy Spirit. Until that time, the yoke of allegiance to the old man or sin nature is a binding force on the will which can be broken only at Calvary.

Satan, the author of the sin nature, has direct access to the innermost part of the unbeliever, his spirit. Thus, the alien life within has a supply source which is inexhaustible in quantity, though its quality can never compare with that available in the Lord Jesus Christ. Some may have marveled at the involvement of otherwise brilliant people in various aspects of occult phenomena. It would seem that they, of all people, should know better; but they are merely being consistent with their nature which, like those in the days of Noah, is "only evil continually" (Genesis 6:5). The supernatural power manifested by those in some forms of the occult is mute testimony to the fact that spiritual power (from the Enemy) is operating in the individual. Such a person can, indeed, be very "spiritual"; the problem is that the power is from the wrong spirit!

The unbeliever also receives support from without from the world system, which is consistent with his nature since Satan is also the god of this world or cosmos. This means that the well-adjusted unbeliever who is not under conviction of the Holy Spirit is living a life of seeming equilibrium; his inner being is in harmony with his environment. If he is psychologically well adjusted he may live for years in this condition until God begins to close in on him in answer to the prayer and witness of interested Christians.

As he begins to consider his situation in light of eternity, there begins to be an unrest with which he has no resources to cope. The God-sized vacuum within begins to demand the satisfaction that can be supplied only through a personal relationship with the Lord Jesus Christ.

The Carnal or Fleshly Man

The typical person who trusts the Lord Jesus Christ as Savior does not go on into the victory that comes through abiding in Christ. Instead, the new birth may result in more internal conflict than the person previously described has ever experienced. This sounds like a contradiction in terms, since a personal relationship with the Lord Jesus Christ is propounded as the source of peace—not of conflict. Certainly, in the ideal situation, more serious conflict is not the result! However, to invite the Lord Jesus into the life and refuse to yield the life to his total control is but to set the stage for strife. Suddenly, a balanced situation no longer exists. The core of his being, the regenerated spirit, or new man, is now at odds with the world system and his former pattern of living. Both of these have him programmed to go in the opposite direction to that in which his new nature will now tug him. This is an apt description of the carnal or fleshly man depicted by Diagram 3. Such a person has been regenerated or has had a spiritual birth through trusting Christ as Savior and Lord. He has "put off . . . the old man" (Ephesians 4:22) and thus has a new nature or new man which is indwelt by the Holy Spirit. However, his soul—and consequently his behavior—is dominated by the power of indwelling sin (not by the old man). It is as though there were a barrier (depicted by the heavy black rim) between his spirit and his soul which effectually prevents the Holy Spirit from controlling or filling him (Ephesians 5:18) through his spirit's being in the ascendancy over his soul. The area representing

CARNAL OR FLESHLY MAN

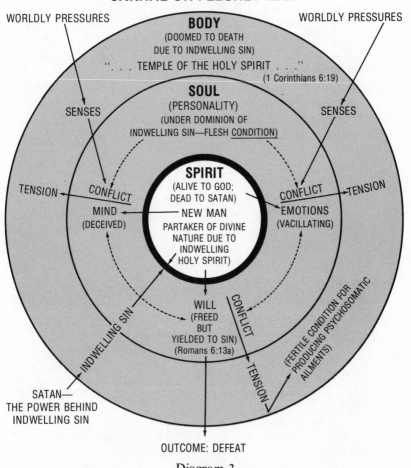

Diagram 3

the soul is shaded to depict the condition known as "flesh" or "self"—the personality under the dominion of indwelling sin.

The carnal man is ineffective both on the human and the spiritual plane. As depicted by the opposing arrows between spirit and soul, he is "grieving the Spirit" (*see* Ephesians 4:30) and is not fully yielded either to indwelling sin or to the indwelling Spirit. Since a man cannot serve two masters, there will be an unrelenting struggle for mastery by the Holy Spirit; refusal to yield to the control of the Spirit can result in emotional and/or mental symptoms ranging all the way from defeat in the Christian life to neurotic or psychotic disorders. The functions of mind, will, and emotions are much the same as described in Diagram 2. This mind is deceived in that it responds more to sense data than to the promptings of the Holy Spirit and the Word of God. This is due to past programming by the world system and the continued operation of the power of indwelling sin. Though his spirit is no longer affected by the power of sin and cannot respond to it in that he "died unto sin" (Romans 6:10), his soul—having been a slave to sin through the old man prior to regeneration—has been conditioned to respond to and cooperate with the power of indwelling sin (the *condition* of "flesh").

The emotions, as described in Diagram 2, are more or less caught between the *will* and the *mind*; the emotions are neither damaged nor healed *directly*. The mind functions in the role of intermediary, and those hurts to the emotions are first perceived in the mind—except in the case of a very young child, when such basic emotions as fear appear to be experienced directly in the emotions.

Diagram 3 depicts the emotions as vacillating, since the conflict between the essential nature of the believer, which is now spiritual, and the soul in the "flesh" *condition* does not permit the emotions to be under the continual control of the indwelt spirit. "For the flesh lusteth against the Spirit, and the Spirit against the flesh: and these are contrary the one to the other: so that ye cannot do the things that ye would" (Galatians 5:17). Thus, the emotions vacillate between the control of the power of indwelling sin in the body and the Holy Spirit through man's spirit.

The fact that the old man has been crucified (Romans 6:6) and replaced by the new man or regenerated spirit renders the *will* free to choose between the control of indwelling sin and the Holy Spirit. However, the sense data perceived by the mind is in total contradiction to the revealed Word of God. Also, the damage sustained in the emotions during the developmental years tends to further deny the truth of freedom of choice in the *will*. The power of indwelling sin continues to cause the mind to work under deception and to reinforce the negative emotions. Thus, the soul is caught in continual tension between the spirit which is indwelt by the Holy Spirit and worldly pressures induced by indwelling sin and its author, Satan, combined with the environmental conditions (also influenced by the Enemy of Souls).

The conflict in the soul results in tension in the body which may instigate psychosomatic ailments. Resolution of such conflict is to be found in yielding to the lordship of Jesus Christ and thereby becoming a spiritual man. Diagram 4 represents the spiritual man, whose soul or personality is under control of the indwelling Holy Spirit, with resulting harmony in his entire being.

Spiritual Man

Since the spiritual man is controlled and led by the Spirit, he is functioning in harmony with God and accomplishing God's purpose for his life. He is crucified to the world and the world is crucified to him through the Lord Jesus Christ (Galatians 6:14). However, the effect of sin on the body will still make its destination the grave until the believer ultimately receives a glorified body and is free from the presence of sin, as well as from its penalty and power.

The mind has been renewed according to Romans 12:2, and the will has appropriately yielded (Romans 6:13) to the truth assimilated by the enlightened mind; the result is that the emotions are controlled by the Holy Spirit and the fruit of the

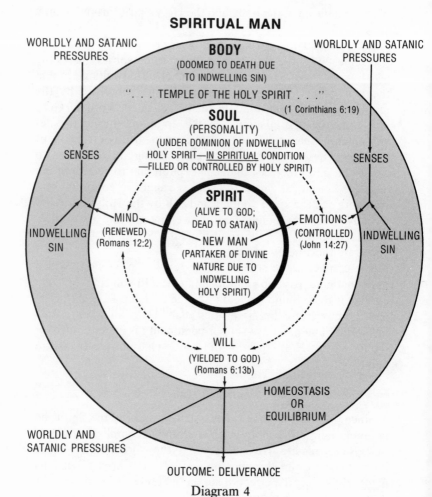

Diagram 4

Spirit—love, joy, peace, etc. (Galatians 5:22, 23)—is manifested through the life. The soul is under the control of the spirit, with the body also being quickened by the indwelling Holy Spirit (Romans 8:11). The result is a harmonious working together of the constituent parts of man. Although sin still indwells and worldly and Satanic pressures abound, the Spirit-controlled believer is appropriating his resources in Christ to walk in victory over the world, the flesh, and the devil.

God's Purpose for the Believer

God's goal for redeemed man is that he ". . . be conformed to the image of his Son . . ." (Romans 8:29). The new birth is a crisis in that it is a discrete event occurring at a point in time; being conformed to the image of Christ is a process through which the discipline of the Holy Spirit makes us more like the Lord Jesus Christ.

When the adversities are viewed in the light of God's goal for us, we understand that they are our friends (Psalms 119:71), to humble, break, and crush us that the fragrance of the Lord Jesus might emanate from us. We can cooperate with what God is bringing about in our lives, praise Him, and profit by it—or we can resist His gracious chastening (Hebrews 12:11) and defer or abort His will for us.

We can have the abundant life that He promised (John 10:10) as we choose to "walk in the Spirit" (Galatians 5:16)—or we can quench the Spirit (1 Thessalonians 5:19) and, by default, "fulfil the lust of the flesh" (Galatians 5:16b). Our choice determines our lot on planet Earth: we can exist—or *live*. Having not chosen to walk *in the Spirit,* we have automatically chosen to walk *after the flesh.* Such a choice has set us on a collision course with God's will by frustrating His purpose for our lives.

The resulting turmoil makes one a prime candidate for spiritual consultation to determine how adjustment to God's plan and purpose may be brought to pass in the life. It is the overview of this process, along with some steps along the way, that will be covered in the next chapter.

4

Spirituotherapy in Process

A person who enters counseling is not viewed as a patient in need of treatment but as a person with needs requiring spiritual consultation. The symptoms which prompt a person to seek help may range from vocational dissatisfaction to marital discord to severe mental and emotional disturbances. All of these and those in between that are functional as opposed to organic in nature have their roots in the lack of a viable relationship with God through the Lord Jesus Christ.

This is not to say that all symptoms or problems are a result of overt sin or that the person is not regenerated. Indeed, the majority of mental and emotional symptoms have roots traceable to childhood rejection which has limited the person's options in coping with responsibility and stress. The Christian who is not in the vocation or profession for which God has uniquely prepared him is out of God's perfect will for his life and may not have the spiritual acumen to determine the problem or the solution. Thus, frustration and various compensatory behaviors may drive him further from the answer. The person with emotions damaged by rejection has less natural equipment than God intended that he have, not to mention his ignorance or obstinacy in tapping into his spiritual resources in Christ.

As depicted in chapter 3, frustration of God's purpose for an individual—first in coming to Christ and then walking in Christ (Colossians 2:6)—is the prime source of frustration and conflict within the person. The natural man is always at odds with God, so it is just a matter of individual makeup, environment, and choice as to how the resultant conflict will shape the individual's personality and temporal destiny. He is a slave to his sin nature, which is perpetually at enmity with God. Attempts to aid such a person in reducing psychological conflict without introducing him to the Lord Jesus Christ would be merely to comfort him on his way to hell. The true problem is the spiritual conflict with God, not the turmoil which results in the soul or personality.

In the believer the psychological conflict may be much the same, but the source is different. Both have in common the power of indwelling sin, but each takes a different path. Galatians 5:17 tells us that the conflict is between flesh and the Spirit, not between the sin nature and the Spirit. The conflict remains spiritual in nature, with probable psychological conflict being an effect and not a cause. Since this is the case, diagnosis and naming of the psychological symptoms and prescribing treatment of the same are contraindicated. The symptom may be assuaged to some extent or brought to extinction without the spiritual malady having been identified.

The first order of business is to meet the person where he is and manifest the love of Christ to him. In order to love him intelligently he must be understood in all aspects of his life and relationships. This necessitates knowing his personal history as well as his present dilemma. Once understood, it can be related to him in such a manner as to put his life into perspective from a psychological and interpersonal viewpoint. When this information has been communicated to and assimilated by the individual, it is time to proceed to integrate it with the spiritual perspective. Diagrams 5 and 6 have been singularly blessed of the Lord in relating the psychological, physiological, and sociological aspects of the individual's life to his spiritual nature and God's general and specific will.

Although differential diagnosis or specific determination of the psychological problem is not only unnecessary but undesirable and possibly harmful (when the person is given a psychological label), it is of utmost importance that the spiritual condition of the individual be subjected to the analysis of the Holy Spirit. The counselor or spiritual guide can be a catalyst and sounding board as the individual opens himself to God's spiritual microscope.

There are three basic areas of interest in this process:

1. The specific crisis or problem which resulted in the individual's seeking help.
2. Determination of spiritual condition and the stage or plateau of spiritual development of a believer.
3. Obstacles or hindrances to moving in the direction of spiritual growth.

The Presenting Problem

The *presenting problem* (or reason that the person actually gives for seeking help) may be of a marital, psychological, financial, or other nature. Generally speaking, this is a sincere judgment on the part of the person and represents the situation as he sees it. The typical counselor would focus on this and render help in the area of felt need. To be sure, if a person is extremely depressed he definitely needs to be free of depression; the point in question is whether the depression is a problem for resolution or a symptom denoting a deeper problem. The cause of the depression might be unearthed by analysis or other method of therapy. Such cause could be a divorce situation, financial stress, unemployment, guilt, etc. The depression could be alleviated in some cases by electroshock therapy, but the underlying situation would still be extant. Or a job for the unemployed person could eliminate the cause, if we are dealing only with surface issues. The deeper problem to be faced is why the person did not have adequate spiritual resources to handle the unemployment situation and trust God to supply him employment in line with God's will for his life at that point. Getting at the root cause cannot be done on a humanistic level, but all of the aforementioned components must be evaluated and understood in light of the spiritual progress of the individual in question. As this is done the problem area must be fitted into the total scheme of things, that the person may begin to see how God is using this particular situation to shape his life and further his spiritual progress. Helping him to escape this dilemma could be but to impede his spiritual growth, since he would not realize the ultimate outcome that God had intended by permitting the set of circumstances to come to pass in his life. If this situation passes without having accomplished its purpose, God must set about to engineer another, and perhaps more difficult, set of circumstances through which to continue the process of conforming His child to the image of Christ (Romans 8:29).

Since God's overall method of dealing with the individual is to deal with the self-life, and the Cross is the only instrument with which to do it, we place ourselves between the person and God and inhibit His working when we attempt to remove the Cross as it is being applied to the person's life. Galatians 6:2 admonishes us to bear one another's burdens, but we are not to lift the burden or cross totally from the one with whom God is dealing or we become an accomplice in subverting God's plan for his life. Changing the circumstances, geography, marriage partner, job, etc., serves merely to prolong the agony through a temporary respite from suffering.

We might use the example of literal crucifixion as an illustration of alleviated suffering and its dire results. Let's suppose that a person were actually crucified and was writhing in agony on the cross as his life was being snuffed out. He is obviously in pain, physiologically and psychologically, and the pain may be heightened as he approaches his certain death. Although his demise is inevitable, some altruistic souls wish to befriend him and alleviate his suffering. To do so, he is taken down from the cross and has his wounds dressed, is given blood transfusions, water and nourishment, and subsequently nailed again to the cross. This could be done repeatedly and greatly lengthen the agony to be endured during the process of crucifixion. In like manner, we can be doing a grave injustice to a person we long to help by intervening in the circumstances which, rightly understood, could speedily bring to an end the reign of the self-life and inaugurate the freedom and power of resurrection life. May God deliver us from delivering others through human intervention, that the Spirit of God might accomplish the deliverance that only He can consummate.

Determination of Stage of Spiritual Development or Growth

Once the current problem area or crisis has been evaluated in the context of God's dealing with the individual, it is time to assess the person's relationship to God and to plot his spiritual progress. It goes without saying that the first order of business is to determine whether the person is regenerated or not. Once this is formally established, soundings may be taken to fathom spiritual depth.

The counselor may have the witness of the Spirit that the individual is born again but there may be little or no assurance on the part of the believer. If a problem involving assurance is unearthed, it is necessary to determine its origin. A person with such a problem may doubt his salvation, in which event it is a mental or intellectual problem; or, he may "feel unsaved"—a condition which is situate in the emotions. Many otherwise well-taught Christians have been plagued with "feeling unsaved" throughout their Christian experience. Even those in vocational Christian service are not exempt from such feelings. However, it is usually dealt with as a cognitive or intellectual problem—with the person called alongside to help going through the way of salvation from the Bible—it's the umpteenth time the counseled one has heard it. However, since his feelings are frequently at variance with obvious and undeniable facts, they are hardly likely to line up with the facts of Scripture. Understanding of this discrepancy between facts and feeling can frequently pave the way for dealing with the self-life, where the problem actually lies.

Intellectual doubts can be instigated by the enemy, Satan, who is ever alert to continue his program to undermine the Word of God and cast aspersions on God's character. This can happen to any Christian but particularly to those who are committed to go on to possess their possessions in Christ. It is the Christian who is on the front line who is most likely to be singled out for some special attention by the Enemy of Souls. Those who absent themselves from the battle avoid the rigors and suffering of warfare but neither are they partakers of the spoils—the fruit of the Spirit (Galatians 5:22, 23) which accompany the victorious life.

Once the mental and emotional components are considered, the Word is held out to the individual as the only valid premise on which to base assurance—either of salvation or any other aspect of the spiritual life.

The next area to come under scrutiny is the individual's security in his salvation. Until the believer gets his security nailed down he is unlikely to go on to find rest in Christ. If he is insecure he must keep working to maintain his salvation; as long as he works and strives it is patently impossible to rest! It might be well to note at this point that entering into rest regarding salvation does not carry the notion of resting from work; it does mean working from the standpoint of rest! Just as we do not work to get salvation (Ephesians 2:8, 9), neither do we work to maintain it; it is Christ that works in and through us because we are saved. Never should anyone get the idea that the spiritual life is a life of passivity; on the contrary, much more can be done with much less effort. Just as in the matter of assurance, the security of the believer must be anchored solidly in the Word of God, not on fluctuating or damaged emotions.

Another cardinal point to be considered by and with the individual is the matter of his acceptance in Christ. All who are born again have accepted Christ, but the greater percentage of them are ignorant of or cannot accept their acceptance in Christ. Since their emotions have been shaped by an environment of rejection, in the main, it is not incongruous that it should carry over into their spiritual lives. If they have not been accepted by their parents, whom they have seen, how can they possibly understand their acceptance by their heavenly Father, whom they have not seen? The reasoning goes (in their emotions): I feel so unacceptable to those who should love me here on Earth; how can I possibly be accepted by or acceptable to a holy God? All of this despite the fact that they solidly stand on the infallible Word of God and know (intellectually) that they are "accepted in the beloved" (Ephesians 1:6). This is further buttressed by passages such as Ephesians 2:6, which clearly states that He ". . . hath raised us up together, and made us sit together in heavenly places in Christ Jesus," and Colossians 3:3, which avows that our ". . . life is hid with Christ in God." Since these be true and He is accepted by the Father, it follows logically that the individual is accepted by the Father *in Him*. The person who truly understands and appropriates his acceptance in Christ knows that he is of infinite worth as to his self-concept, since the price of his redemption was the blood of Christ—thereby making him worthy to be seated in Christ at the Father's right hand. Hence, the person who has felt and counted himself as absolutely worthless comes to see himself as God sees him.

Likewise, the person who relegates himself to the company of the inept, inadequate, and powerless to produce even on a mere human level comes to understand by divine revelation or enlightenment that it "is Christ in you, the hope of glory" (Colossians 1:27). Ephesians 1:19, 20 tells us that the same power the Father used in raising the Lord Jesus Christ from the dead is available *in us!* Or, since all things were created by and for the Lord Jesus Christ and He holds all things together (Colossians 1:16, 17), His presence within us can harness all that power to produce or perform! With God holding such an exalted opinion of us and meting out His very presence and power within us, how dare we reject ourselves and deprecate our ability to fulfill His calling for us!

A believer who is deficient in his understanding and/or appropriation of his acceptance in Christ will constantly be striving for it or deploring the lack of it in his life. Hence, it is of utmost importance that he come to know that he is accepted and acceptable in Christ. He can intellectually understand the scriptural teaching, but the freedom to be realized as the Spirit teaches this truth is concomitant with his appropriation of his identification with Christ, based upon his total commitment or abandonment to Him—which is our next topic for consideration.

There is widespread misunderstanding as to the meaning of total surrender in that the person often expects some positive change in his life at this point, which may or may not occur. It is imperative that the message get across that it is a decision which will *result* in life changes—*not* the changes *themselves!* Many who have made a solid decision in this regard with no mental reservations have subsequently doubted its validity because it was not immediately and continually corroborated by life-changing experiences. When the person gets the message that this is his permission for God to work on his case, he begins to appreciate why God *has!* Since the positive is frequently preceded by the negative, the person is apt to think that he has failed again in his *effort* to surrender, when such surrender is just what precipitated his probable calamity. The decision will inevitably incur change but may or may not be simultaneous with it.

Once the nature of the commitment is clarified, it is possible for the person to affirm or deny his position relative to it. If such a decision has not been made, we have arrived at the point of departure for our journey in spiritual growth with the individual. If the decision were made at a point in the past, it is necessary to pick up at that point and begin to sort through the salient factors in knowledge and experience to arrive at a mutual understanding of the plateau (or slide) reached, that a benchmark may be established for later reference as we proceed.

The next major point of reference is the understanding and application of the Cross in the life of the individual. If, in answer to queries about the Cross, the reply is couched in terms of Christ's death *for* him, it is obvious that he knows little, if anything, of the operation of the Cross in *his* life. On the contrary, if he relates personal experience regarding his death *with* Christ, it is entirely a different matter. In the former case, he must be led to appropriate by faith his identification with Christ. In the latter case, he already has—and it is necessary to determine just where he is relative to maintenance of victory, spiritual warfare, and service or ministry. Since he is consulting with someone regarding his spiritual life, he has need of information and/or discernment to be prayerfully provided through a mature believer or counselor.

The person may be walking in the Spirit and be desirous of going on in his spiritual growth and service. This being the case, he properly is seeking counsel through another member of the Body who has the gifts needed to be used of the Spirit in his life. The counsel given at this point cannot be predicted or patterned; it will be unique to the situation and tailored by the Spirit to the edification of the individual.

The person who comes bewailing his defeat in life and/or ministry, for which he has no understanding or way out, is an entirely different matter. His walk in Christ since appropriation of Christ as his life must be evaluated in detail to determine the extent of his understanding of the Cross, his appropriation of its power in his life and witness, and his departure from victory. It may be his first major resurgence of the flesh or self after entering into victory, and he must learn the principle of continuous reckoning of himself to be dead to sin and alive unto God (Romans 6:11). With the flesh in operation once more, he may also have been under some Satanic oppression which has resulted in his being deceived with respect to the source of the problem. If depression has been a way of life as he walked after the flesh, he may not recognize the difference between *oppression* and *depression*. In either event, the flesh (or self-life) must be dealt with; depression may lift immediately or gradually, but oppression, at times, must be handled by direct confrontation with the enemy, Satan. James 4:7 gives the method: "Submit yourselves therefore to God. Resist the devil, and he will flee from you." The manifestation of the Enemy may be in generalized forms of oppression or in some more specific phenomena such as infiltration of the thought-life ranging all the way to obsession. The reader should refer to chapter 9 ("The Use of Literature") for books providing more extensive treatment of the subject of Satanic or demonic manifestations. Suffice it to say that spiritual warfare is a spiritual problem and God has provided the armor (Ephesians 6) and the weapon (Hebrews 4:12): the Word of God. It is suggested that the novice refrain from dealing with cases involving demonic activity and that none should major in dealing with symptoms. The core problem is the *flesh*, and this is where the battle will be won or lost; the symptoms emanating from the core must be evaluated, and occasionally dealt with directly, but the source must *always* be de-energized.

After the symptoms have been evaluated and the point of departure established, the application by faith of the Cross to the flesh, along with choosing to walk in the Spirit (Galatians 5:16), will gradually or suddenly restore the person to victory. It is not to be expected that emotional relief or release will always accompany a return to claiming victory by faith through reckoning. Otherwise, it would not be necessary to walk by faith—we could *exult* by feeling.

It is often helpful to assist the person in diagraming or mapping his spiritual journey. Dates and events may be identified and placed in proximity to the significant data points. The result will be a testimony in diagrammatic form which may be used for later reference as counseling proceeds and for the individual's establishing of a framework from which to work with others in like manner.

In summary, the constructs are developed and arranged into a framework or pattern which is meaningful to the person. He then evaluates, with the aid of the counselor, his understandings and experience relative to each. Once he, under the direction of the Holy Spirit, has positioned himself in his spiritual growth pattern, he is ready for prayerful consideration of the next step to be taken in faith under the direction and by the empowering of the Holy Spirit.

Obstacles or Hindrances to Movement in Counseling

As counseling proceeds under the direction of the Holy Spirit, intellectual understanding should be accompanied by appropriation by faith of those truths unfolded from the Scripture. Corresponding changes should begin to be manifested in the life; or, said another way, there should be movement or spiritual enlightenment in the life of the person. Should such changes not be evidenced in the individual's life, pause should be given for consideration as to what is blocking the flow of the life of Christ within the person.

Some of the blocks or hindrances to progress are as follows:

Not regenerated.   Although a person may say all the right words by way of testimony, it may be found that a decision was made (intellectual assent) or that an emotional experience occurred but regeneration was not a reality. Caution should be exercised that a person who has the propensity to "feel unsaved" is not confirmed in his lack of assurance. The counselor must depend largely on the witness of the Spirit within, since the words used by the individual may not convey the true picture. This is the most obvious of the list to the uninitiated, since the lack of spiritual birth certainly precludes spiritual growth and development.

Not surrendered.   A person may go through the motions but not really make a firm decision. This is not to say that the decision must be accompanied by emotion, but it must be a firm resolve on which the person follows through— both on the suggestions of the counselor and the injunctions of the Scripture. When either or both are missing, there is good reason to believe that the "surrender" was not valid. If the surrender were purported to have taken place prior to the onset of counseling, the historical record should be closely scrutinized for developments which would support or deny its validity. Reaffirmation of a surrender is not fraught with the same dangers as "accepting

Christ" again. Surrender is a crisis or discrete event coupled with a continued and continual yielding, where regeneration, once a reality, is never repeated.

Unconfessed sin. Known sin which has not been confessed and forsaken will come between the believer and God (Isaiah 59:2), destroy fellowship, and prevent further growth. Some sins may require acknowledgement to another individual, such as a spiritual counselor, before the individual can forgive himself, accept God's forgiveness, or successfully repent and turn from them.

Restitution. Harm done to another must be rectified, where possible, in the Lord's timing, or it can interfere with fellowship and spiritual growth. Asking and granting forgiveness of those known to be offended or to have offended us may also be a necessity (Matthew 5:23, 24).

Critical or unforgiving spirit. A spirit of resentment or bitterness which has not been faced and dealt with will also hinder progress.

Fear. This is all-pervasive, ubiquitous emotion which underlies most, if not all, resistance to the counseling process. Loss of face with the counselor or other important persons in one's life can prevent openly dealing with all issues. Many fear what God will do to them if they yield all rights to Him, even though they know their fear is irrational. Loss of material possessions or of loved ones is frequently given as the reason a person is afraid to sell out to Christ. Some fear losing their minds or having a nervous breakdown, particularly after having gone through one previously. Fear of freedom or of the unknown is very common; the neurotic defenses erected over the years become a type of "security." Many balk at what God may require of them once they have yielded the "right to veto." Some fear that others may think them insincere and that they are being manipulative.

Refusal to break sinful alliances. Exposure of sinful practices and relationships may bring humiliation, unemployment, bankruptcy, imprisonment, loss of lover, or other situations which one cannot face, or refuses to face and terminate.

Perceived rejection by God. A person who has never known acceptance may find it too big a gamble to believe God will accept him; if he tries and "it doesn't work," there is no other place to turn. In his emotions, he is certain that God, too, will reject him.

Betrayal. So many others have betrayed and rejected him that he expects the counselor, others, and God to follow suit.

Lack of faith. Some feel that "too great a miracle" is required in their cases and are afraid to trust God to intervene.

Refusal to suffer. When the mental and emotional pain becomes acute, a person may resort to almost anything to alleviate his pain—drugs, alcohol, illicit relationships, escape from the situation, etc.—these and many other temptations may be overwhelming in their appeal as the end approaches. As previously described, taking steps to relieve the pain will merely prolong the agony. The Cross is never alluring and enticing in its appeal; it is a place to end suffering but not to avoid it.

Emotions must agree. Some do not know they can make a rational choice of faith by the exercise of the will when the feelings or emotions are in contradiction.

Unknown. At times there are blocks from complicated interrelationships of rejection-based emotions which may or may not surface in counseling. Alas, there may be fear dating back to an early-childhood experience which cannot be recalled by the individual. So long as the person is not willingly or knowingly harboring information and/or behavior destructive to his spiritual life, the Spirit of God can and will work around the unknown to release him. In some cases the Holy Spirit will recall to conscious memory events long forgotten which need to be exposed to the Son-light for healing.

Refusal to study.   Since the Word of God is paramount in God's dealing with His children, cutting off this avenue on a willful basis will delay, if not prevent, God's working in the life.

Lack of prayer.   It is important that God talk to the person through the Word; and it is perhaps equally important that the person talk to God in prayer. Since the Holy Spirit is the Therapist, it is mandatory that the person spend time alone with Him in conjunction with the Word.

Fellowship.   Time spent with other believers in study, prayer, and worship—privately and in the context of the Church—is signally important. God frequently ministers the Word in the power of the Spirit through other believers, especially in the Church as His ordained institution, so it behooves the person to avail himself of every opportunity to saturate himself in the Word and in fellowship.

Service.   Refusal to become involved in the spreading of the gospel of the Lord Jesus Christ through a Bible-believing church and affiliated organizations can grieve or quench the Spirit. Some would rather be loners and "do their things" outside the context of the Church. Ministry in Church-related organizations can be very helpful but should never replace involvement and establishment in the local church. Each believer needs a church home and the nurture of pastors who can instruct, admonish, reprove, and rebuke, as necessary, that the believer become established in Christ. Such a relationship with a pastor can be a vital link in growth in Christ and in service.

Summary

When an obstacle to understanding and movement in the counseling process is unearthed, the first order of business is to help the client see what is inhibiting progress. Once a clear intellectual understanding is gained it is necessary to deal with it scripturally, including dealing realistically with any sin involved. Some of the obstacles mentioned here will be identified and resolved readily in the course of the initial hour, as discussed in the next chapter. The more subtle ones, or the strongholds, may take a little more time to ferret out, and this will be the objective of succeeding interviews as described in chapter 6.

5

The Initial Hour

Most of the people who do personal work go through a period of fear and trepidation in approaching an unbeliever to relate to him the good news of the gospel. A structured situation in a church is somewhat easier than going into a home to present the claims of Christ to unsaved people. Also, it is easier to go into a home by invitation than to knock on doors until an opportunity opens to present the gospel.

Once the soul-winning situation is set up, the personal worker is faced with the necessity of having an approach with which he is comfortable and which puts the person with whom he is dealing at ease. Many who would share Christ have more zeal than knowledge and offend more people than they win. The reader may have heard of the barber who was newly saved and was eager to witness to his experience with Jesus Christ. As he met his customer the next day he was sharpening his straight razor on the leather strap. His initial approach to his customer was, "Are you ready to die?" One can imagine what went through the customer's mind as he viewed the finely honed razor. As the cliché goes, if we don't use *tact* we may lose *contact*.

Once we have established contact we need to know where to go from there; this involves an understanding of our goal and the general path we will take to get there while allowing the Holy Spirit to make any deviations He chooses along the way. Canned speeches can be a detriment in a gospel presentation, but abysmal ignorance of hoa to proceed may be even worse!

The counseling as described herein is a specialized approach to personal work which may be utilized with Christians and non-Christians alike. Since the recipient may have some moderate to severe problems, there is the absolute necessity to meet him where he is—both spiritually and psychologically. If this is accomplished in a loving and understanding manner, it will usually take considerably longer than a few minutes at the altar in the rush to finish so the invitation may be closed. Many of those Christians who respond to an invitation have no idea as to what they need, but they do know there is a *need!* A personal worker may do irreparable harm to such a person by merely telling him to get right with God by confessing his sins. He may have confessed his sins times without number without finding the way to victory over the power of sin or the way out of spiritual warfare which he may be encountering. When he is not heard, understood, and helped to understand where he is and how he may appropriate the answer to be found in Christ, he has been subtly rejected as a person. A seeking person must be allowed the dignity of being treated and accepted as a person—then begin together to consider the problematical behavior in the light of God's love and acceptance so that sin may be placed in its proper perspective. God loves and accepts the sinner while ealing radically with his sin. Calvary is at once God's demonstration of His love for the sinner in taking such extreme measures to provide atonement and—in contrast—of His extreme hatred of sin in permitting His only Son to become sin and then venting His wrath upon sin embodied in Him (2 Corinthians 5:21).

The Approach

In meeting the individual and beginning the initial hour it is important that a relationship as equals be established. In other words, the aura of a "professional" relationship is to be avoided like the plague. The insecure counselor or the one who doesn't have God's only complete answer in Jesus Christ must utilize the professional front to insure distance. Thus, he is protected from revealing himself and places himself on a "higher" level where he can operate from an invulnerable platform. In doing so, he elevates himself and leaves the client or "patient" on a lower level in some ways, which means he has effectively "put down" the person from the beginning! How much better it is to begin on the same level as two sinners saved by grace, or as one sinner who has been saved and another who is about to be!

Starting off in such a manner creates trust and rapport almost from the opening remarks in getting acquainted. Once the ice is broken and an open, trusting relationship is established, the person doesn't feel "put down" but accepted; and the way is paved to look at some attitudes and behaviors which may be totally unacceptable to God *and,* frequently, to the person relating the transgressions.

Usually, it is good to begin by inquiring into the nature of the problem which eventuated in the person's seeking spiritual counsel. This could be in the nature of a marital problem, emotional/mental disturbances, children with problems, among a host of others. Suicide is frequently an imminent solution which is among the alternatives that have been considered. This problem or crisis faced by the individual is sometimes called the *presenting problem* in counseling circles; it is the situation he *presents* or puts forward as the problem. Once the press of this particular problem has been understood by the counselor it is time to move on to the larger picture of seeing this problem in the context of the whole life.

This is accomplished by securing the life story of the individual in a manner conducive to understanding the present difficulty in the light of significant past events. The author has found it advantageous to retrace the person's life history from birth to date in outline form while noting significant data which have had a significant impact during the developmental stages of his life. This history taking would generally occupy the first twenty to twenty-five minutes of the counseling hour. Notes should be taken during the time of securing the life history, especially when the counselor is seeing new clients almost daily. Discretion should be used in the information committed to paper lest confidential information fall into the wrong hands through theft or accident. The notes are also helpful in keeping track of commitments and progress and for the eventuality that another staff counselor might see the client in an emergency situation. Significant rejections occurring in childhood on into teenage years are the key criteria in setting the stage for damaged emotions. Likewise, traumatic events causing inordinate fear or guilt can play a significant role in shaping a person's emotional life. The way a person thinks of himself (usually known as his *self-concept*) and the reasons behind such thinking will usually emerge rather rapidly as the rejection syndrome comes into focus.

The familiarization with the person's history may be secured along the following lines. The key questions below are in the chronological order generally utilized; thorough acquaintance with the sequence will enable the reader to follow and utilize the history-taking method with little difficulty.

1. Are your parents living?
2. If so, are they living together?
3. If one or both died or they are separated, what age were you at the time?
4. If such changes took place, where or with whom did you live afterward?
5. Was this the only marriage for your parents?
6. How many siblings (brothers and sisters) in your immediate family? Where do you fit in? How many years difference between you and those siblings immediately younger and older?
7. If a stepparent were involved, how were you treated? Compare your treatment with that of stepbrothers and stepsisters by the stepparent.
8. If you had to leave the parental home, what was your living situation? How did you feel about it? Were one or all siblings with you?

9. As a child, were you closer to your mom or to your dad? Which could you talk to about threatening matters, if either?

10. Did either parent express or show love?

11. Was favoritism shown to other siblings?

12. Do you vividly recall any significant happenings—bad or good—prior to beginning school?

13. Were you ever sexually molested? At what age? By same sex or opposite sex? Someone your age or adult? Did you ever tell anyone about it? How long after it occurred?

14. How did you relate to siblings? Was there jealousy?

15. Were either or both of your parents overprotective? Describe.

16. From the ages of 6 to 12, were you outgoing? Withdrawn? Happy? Sad?

17. How many close friends from ages 6 to 12?

18. Were there any significant changes in your attitudes toward yourself or others during junior high school? Significant events?

19. What were you like during high school? When did you start dating? Any steadies?

20. What about sexual development and relationships during high school? Same or opposite sex? Guilt over self-stimulation?

21. Did you complete high school?

22. What did you do after high school? College? Military service? Any combat? Work?

23. At what age were you married? Children? If that marriage failed, at what age? Subsequent marriages? Children and/or stepchildren?

24. Describe the marriage(s).

25. What kind of work or study are you in at present?

26. What is your emotional and mental state at the present time? Any physiological symptoms?

27. Have you ever been in therapy? When? What kind? How long? Prescribed drugs at present?

28. Any problems, past or present, with drugs or alcohol?
29. If married, how is sexual adjustment?
30. Are there any excessive financial pressures at this time? Do you and spouse agree on money management?
31. What is the psychological and social health of your children at this time?
32. Describe communication with spouse.
33. Do you have a relationship with God? How established? At what age? Are you currently affiliated with a church? What kind? Are you regular in attendance? Active in ministry?
34. What do you see as the chief problem which must be resolved?
35. Do you feel you are open to God's solution?

Upon securing the answers to the queries above, the basic data is in the possession of the counselor to have the needed understanding of the individual as the basis for proceeding to tie it together for the client and proceed in orderly fashion to present the answer. The questions above are not intended to be fired at the unsuspecting individual in machine-gunlike fashion. These merely serve as a repertoire for gleaning information not voluntarily divulged in the course of the get-acquainted portion of the first interview.

The person should feel totally free to talk, with little interruption by the counselor except for clarification. Appropriate questions may usually be inserted without derailing the person's train of thought. Many persons have had a steady diet of being preached at and taught at, so that there is a great need to be heard and understood in an accepting environment. Indeed, an occasional person talks so compulsively one would think he had been vaccinated with a phonograph needle! Very infrequently, it is necessary for such a person to talk unrelentingly for the whole hour; when the need is there, it would be rejection to force him to do otherwise.

Once the history is taken in this manner, the *presenting*

problem has been identified and there is usually some indication as to whether the person is a Christian. At times, it will also be possible to discern with some degree of accuracy as to the stage of spiritual development. Since the ultimate answer is spiritual, it is self-evident that the basic problem is spiritual also. Therefore, continual assessment is in order to determine the stage of spiritual growth and obstacles or hindrances to growth. In other words, an ongoing spiritual diagnosis is necessary if the proper spiritual counsel is to be given. Understanding of the psychological symptoms can be an aid in understanding the individual, but labeling the emotional and/or mental symptoms can be very detrimental to acceptance of God's answer in Christ. Many persons have studied psychology texts exhaustively and have found that their particular label has a very poor prognosis from the viewpoint of conventional therapy. It is most reassuring to an individual to find a counselor who takes no stock in such labels or prognoses made by experts in the world system.

A young lady who was married and had a small son had experienced much trauma and was referred to one of the best-known and respected psychiatric centers in the United States. After a complete psychiatric workout, her husband was told that she was manic-depressive and that there was no hope. He was advised to put her in an institution, get a divorce, and start a new life. This could be rather depressing news when coming from the acknowledged experts in the field! However, he refused their advice and their prognosis and availed his wife of spiritual counsel. Living in the home of a spiritual counselor for a week resulted in the Spirit of God releasing her from most of the symptomatology and restoration to her home and family. When the counselor can sit face to face with such a troubled person and discount with confidence past labels and predictions and state with confident faith born of experience that this and all other needs can be met in the Lord Jesus Christ, his faith is contagious.

Having elicited all of the above data, it is necessary to tie it all together for the person to help him see how past trauma and rejection is causing present disturbances and/or behavior. Those who have been rejected tend to operate from a framework of rejection such that they tend to engender rejection on the part of others. The rejection syndrome should be simply explained to him, since many who have been rejected have never recognized it as such. An explanation of the feelings it causes and the behaviors it prompts can be done in two to five minutes, with great insight being gained by the client in most cases. Thus, present psychological and social adjustments can be clearly shown to be a result of antecedent events and conditions. It isn't absolutely necessary for a person to be armed with this understanding to appropriate the answer in Christ, but it is comforting to him to know there are usually rational explanations for irrational behavior that he can understand. Once understood, he is no longer shadowboxing but grappling with predictable emotional responses from past programming, however distant.

When interviewing a couple, it is best to take a general history of the relationship from the beginning, much as you would the history of an individual. After the history and condition of the relationship have been assessed, the counselor can interview the individuals separately as previously described. Frequently there are things in the past or present lives of the individuals which have never been divulged to the other. Some of those things may never need to be said to the spouse, but there should always be the openness to the Holy Spirit's direction in such matters. Once the couple has been interviewed together and separately (usually in that order), the counselor can move on to an explanation of the test and to a cohesive presentation of the answer, as described in the next few pages.

To assist in his intellectual understanding of his present condition, it has been found that the Taylor-Johnson Temperament Analysis (Psychological Publications, 5300 Hollywood Blvd., Los Angeles, CA 90027) can be an invaluable tool. There is an educational prerequisite to being able to receive training and purchase the materials to use the test, but most pastors and counselors would qualify. The results of this test are profiled relative to nine significant traits such as nervousness, depression, and hostility. Other tests may be utilized but the simplicity of this one, along with the fact that it is economical and can be hand scored, commend it for this use. It is not the purpose of this test to diagnose "mental illness," nor is it the purpose of the counselor to do therapy based upon it. It merely acts as a self-descriptive tool to aid one in understanding himself and how others see him.

Those traits stemming from rejection picked up earlier in the interview may usually be very easily plugged in to the results of this test. Upon completion of the explanation of this test to the client, a transition statement is suggested, such as "Now let's look at how all of this fits together and the answer which God has provided to meet these needs." The Wheel diagram (#5) provides an excellent tool whereby intrapersonal relationships may be explained in a simple manner which points up self or flesh as the root cause of problems in the Christian.

Up to this point, the information given by the client has been necessarily very brief. It is an overall view of what he has experienced and what he is at present experiencing. Subsequent interviews will serve the purpose of filling in the details. The brevity is absolutely essential if the person is to leave at the end of the hour with the knowledge that there *is* an answer and, as a minimum, an intellectual understanding *of* that answer. Those who have frequented the offices of psychiatrists say with monotonous regularity, "He never told me anything; he just let me do all the talking." It would be a travesty if a person left after an hour with a spiritual counselor with the same impression! That infrequent client who must talk the whole hour should be shown the necessity of a return appointment at the earliest possible time (preferably within twenty-four hours), that he might be shown God's way out.

It will take twenty to twenty-five minutes for the experienced counselor to do an adequate job of reviewing the Wheel and Line diagrams with an individual. Just as the information was extracted in brief form because of the press of time, the answer will be given in like manner. The first hour is designed to give overall spiritual and psychological understanding upon which to build in succeeding counseling hours and in the individual's study.

In proceeding through the Wheel diagram, it should be kept in mind that basic constructs or concepts are to be taught with the client's understanding of—and relationship to—each concept being established prior to advancing to the next. A straight "presentation" might miss the mark in many areas without the counselor's having known it. The client should be vitally involved in the explanation through questions from the counselor, and with questions from the client being invited. However, questions must be limited to those which are germane or it will be impossible to relate all of the necessary information in the allotted time. Also, the temptation to enlarge on the spiritual truths involved should be resisted because too much input in one interview can be counterproductive.

It is essential to explain the makeup of man with particular reference to the definition of the "soul" or personality and the distinctions between the soul and the spirit. The client should indicate understanding of this vital point before moving on to the functions of each and their interrelationships.

If antagonism to spiritual things is detected or suspected it may be well to brush lightly the concepts under "spirit" with some comment such as "This refers to a personal relationship with God" and move on to a discussion of the items under "soul," with which the client will readily identify in most cases. After having seen that the counselor can explain his psychological and related physiological difficulties, most clients are willing to take a look at the spiritual implications. It must be remembered that most people have years of conditioning to preclude their seeing psychological *symptoms* as *spiritual* problems. For instance, a young fellow about eight years of age came for counseling and his presenting problem was that of having defecated in his pants five or six times a day. Now let's face it, most parents wouldn't take their children to the pastor in such circumstances! However, after one

Diagram 5

interview with the counselor, he had one "accident" in one week. Many adults have the same problem (spastic colon) but they are able to recognize the symptoms earlier and run faster!

With the average client, it is possible to move through the Wheel pretty much as described here and in the Appendix. In using the Wheel diagram, the word *salvation* should be explained in gross terms to see if the client readily relates to it; if not, a thorough explanation should usually be withheld until the Line diagram can be utilized with the appropriate Scriptures near the end of the hour. The counselor should have some indication by this time as to whether or not he is dealing with a Christian.

The term *assurance* deserves some attention here since it is a common malady to lack it on the part of many Christians. There are both intellectual and emotional components involved; a person may *know* he is saved and yet *feel* unsaved. Doubting salvation is intellectual whereas "feeling unsaved" is emotionally based.

Because of widespread misunderstanding of the meaning of *total commitment*, this term should be explained very clearly before the client commits himself about his position relative to it. A faulty conception of total commitment has been a hang-up in the lives of many regarding spiritual growth. Some have said to the Lord, "I'll do anything You want me to do!"; others have surrendered to preach; and yet others have surrendered to the mission field. Many of these still lack that which is needful—total abandonment of all rights to themselves! Some confuse total commitment with vocational Christian service, while others confuse it with the *results* of total commitment—a renewed mind (Romans 12:2) and a transformed life.

The next concept to be established is that of *self* (later to be clarified as synonymous with *flesh*). Since most persons entering counseling have never considered the makeup of man in detail, it is best to build the constructs simply and then expand, as necessary, in subsequent interviews.

The constructs under the "Soul" portion of the Wheel are to be thoroughly explained with the additional proviso that information obtained earlier in the hour during history taking should be fitted in as appropriate to personalize it for the individual. For instance, the client may have hit something or someone as the result of frustration; this can easily be shown as the manner in which he released his hostility, possibly accompanied by some dramatics as the counselor describes it. Once the functioning (or dysfunctioning) of the personality is understood with concomitant psychophysiological (or psychosomatic) symptoms, as shown in Diagram 5, some summary statements are in order to emphasize that symptoms in both body and soul hearken back to the source—self. This point being clearly made, it is time to explain the Line Diagram (#6) to see how God deals with the problem (self, along with accompanying sins), and thereby resolves intrapersonal and interpersonal conflicts. (See Appendix.)

In addition to covering substitutionary aspects of the Cross thoroughly for the unsaved, it is vital to establish a clear understanding of the meaning of eternal life, considering our life *in Adam* and our life *in Christ.* With some persons it gives great freedom to understand what they were in Adam and how the Cross dealt with that; with others, the truth of our identification with Christ in death and resurrection is the salient truth; and with yet others it is the truth of being seated, acceptable, and *accepted* in Christ at the right hand of God (Ephesians 1:6 and 2:6). Eternal life has only a present and future dimension in the understanding of the great majority of Christians; the line is intended to show them their eternal past as well as their eternal future.

Once these points are clearly made and intellectually understood, it is time to see if the Holy Spirit has taught, convicted, and convinced the person that he must act on the truth that God has shown him. It is at this point that the counselor must trust the Counselor to give discernment as to whether the person has been readied by the Holy Spirit to act on truth by faith, whether or not the emotions are in agreement. If so, he is challenged to make the appropriate commitment. If he is unsaved, it is appropriate to challenge him to trust in the Lord

Jesus Christ as Savior, Lord, and Life. If he has never totally yielded his life to the Lord, he is given the opportunity to do this and to pray, claiming by faith his death, burial, resurrection, and seating with the Lord Jesus Christ, thus being freed by faith from the domination of indwelling sin.

Once the prayer of commitment is made, the person is instructed to look to the facts of God's Word and deny the temptation to check the emotions to see if God did anything, just as in salvation. By faith the transaction has been made, and the changes to be made within the person and in the adverse circumstances are to be *scheduled* and *accomplished* by the Holy Spirit with the continued full cooperation of the person's will. Aggressive yielding of the will is in order—not passively waiting on "something to happen" but walking in faith that what God has promised He is able also to perform (Romans 4:21).

At the close of the interview the client is instructed to review the information covered in the last half of the interview prior to the next interview (usually about a week) and to study Scripture passages assigned. If the person is newly saved he would be supplied a Bible study for new Christians. If he is yet unsaved he should be given whatever material is appropriate to his case to permit him to study the way of salvation from the Word. Some unbelievers will not study the Word but might read a book such as *The Late Great Planet Earth* by Hal Lindsey or something similar. The study assignments will be given more attention in chapters 8 and 9.

It is usually in order for the counselor to open with prayer and trust that by the end of the hour the client will be ready to pray in closing. If hostility is sensed in the beginning it is better to omit prayer than to make a fetish of it and alienate the client from the beginning.

The next interview will routinely be scheduled for about a week unless the person is severely depressed, psychotic, suicidal, or cannot concentrate to apply what has been covered in the first interview. In such cases, massed appointments on a daily basis may be indicated until the Holy Spirit begins to break through and relieve some of the symptoms. The first

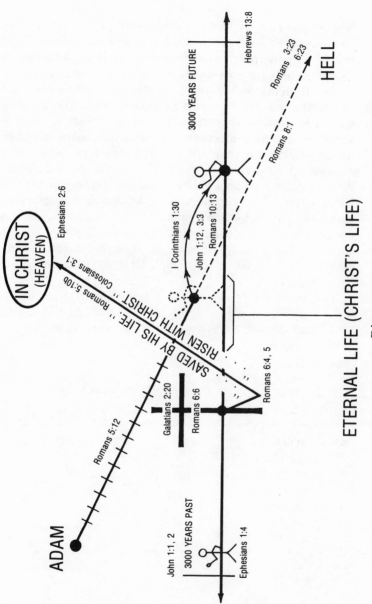

ETERNAL LIFE (CHRIST'S LIFE)

Diagram 6

hour should have yielded from the client the necessary information in brief form and in the impartation of the answer to him in gross terms. Succeeding interviews, as described in chapter 6, will serve to supply detail in both particulars.

The Appendix contains the transcript of an actual interview which is illustrative of the foregoing description of an initial hour. The reader is encouraged to thoroughly familiarize himself with the objectives and procedures delineated in this chapter and then study the Appendix to see how these were exemplified in the counseling hour. The names and some of the details have been changed but the essential data is given just as it transpired. It is a "textbook" case which clearly portrays the concepts and constructs pertaining to the initial hours, and it is commended for modeling the counselor's technique. Though each initial hour will be unique, most of the essential ingredients are to be found in this sample interview or consultation.

6

Succeeding Interviews

In contrast to the first hour of interview, which is highly structured, succeeding interviews may take most any direction under the leadership of the Holy Spirit. The initial hour may also deviate significantly from the plan, but the structure is there from which to deviate.

Rather than lay down any specific information to get or impart, this chapter will suggest some guidelines within which the counselor will usually find himself operating. In general, succeeding counseling hours will fall into a pattern in which there is about half counseling and half teaching. That is, unstructured interaction or conversation with no attempt on the part of the counselor to guide toward any specific objective permits the Holy Spirit to guide into fruitful areas of understanding, both psychologically and spiritually. As the hour unfolds, it will become apparent that some input is needed from the counselor by way of clarification or teaching. However, material will not usually be given the client along predetermined lines. The Holy Spirit understands good education techniques, "For precept must be upon precept, precept upon precept; line upon line, line upon line; here a little, and there a little" (Isaiah 28:10). The counselor himself may be surprised at the turn of events in a counseling hour, as each is put together in a unique fashion.

The interview would generally start out with a casual "Well, what has been happening since you were last here?" This leaves the client free to launch out in any direction he chooses, and the counselor trusts the Holy Spirit to take it from there. Things may be considerably better or worse, depending upon the work God needs to do in the life. The client may have received sufficient psychological and spiritual insight that he wants to talk and put things together. Or he may want to elaborate on details of his past or present life to fill in the skeleton outline covered in the first half of the first interview. It is the counselor's job to see that the client is not rambling on and on after the basic situation has been discussed.

After the client has exhausted all of the things he wants to talk about, within and without, the counselor begins systematically to see where the client is, relative to the data *input* received in the first hour. Queries about his understanding of the spiritual and psychological information portrayed by the Wheel and Line diagrams will usually reveal some areas where additional teaching or clarification is required. As the client reacts to this type of probing, the counselor must be sensitive to the mood and spirit of the client. Is he more or less depressed? More or less hostile? More or less fearful? Is he dealing with the real world? Is he suicidal? Are there any symptoms indicative of a physiological problem? How recently has he had a thorough physical examination? Is he dealing primarily with objective or subjective data? Is he able to concentrate? Does he retain a good percentage of what he hears or reads? These and a hundred other questions will clamor for attention as the effort is made to really get to know where he comes from and where he is.

If any type of commitment were made in the first interview, directly or indirectly, a determination should be made as to whether the commitment were real. If the client trusted Christ, did his reaction to the initial question at the beginning of the interview reveal any signs indicative of new life? Has he told anyone about receiving Christ? Attended church? Has he read the Word? Prayed? Or, if a total surrender of his life occurred, is there any evidence of his letting go of the controls? Did he surrender and appropriate Christ as life? If so, has there been any change in the symptoms he reported during the previous interview? If he truly did business with God, there should be some evidence that God has begun to work on his case! When God begins *His* work there may be an *increase* in the client's discomfort, since God has to do some pruning to make way for new life. Understanding of this on the part of the client can result in his cooperating with God, thus shortening the process; or, he may resist or try to assuage the symptoms by other means (escape, tranquilizers, alcohol, etc.) and delay the process.

As the hour continues, it is imperative to find out (without asking) whether rapport has been established between counselor and client. Usually, the spiritual counselor finds that the Holy Spirit provides this in the first interview. When it is there, the counselor can "say it like it is" without fear of destroying the relationship; when it is not, he must proceed *very carefully!* Much understanding and love is required with some persons to win their trust, since the rejection syndrome has them set up for further rejection. Breaking through the defenses to get to a person to love him can be the greatest hurdle to overcome!

The counselor should constantly be alert to determine the client's commitment to the counseling process. Does he want to work out his problem at any cost (not expressed in terms of money), or is he counting the cost before deciding whether he will permit God to do what is needful? Is he likely to bail out when the going gets rough, or is he committed to see it through to the end (his demise at the cross)? When such commitment is lacking it is unlikely that there will be resolution of the symptoms in evidence in the person's life. Before too much time passes (within two or three interviews at most), this issue should be confronted. It will be a waste of the counselor's time to continue when the person avowedly disclaims any intention of getting serious. Without rejecting the person, it can be decided to delay further counseling until the client is more acutely aware of his need.

Another procedure which can be very revealing as far as

motives and security are concerned is to be aware of whether the client is homing in on symptoms (marriage, job, depression, etc.), or on the problem—the self-life. When he has the proper perspective the symptoms will fade into the background and will be utilized only as a barometer of where he is as he deals with the self-life.

It is vital that the study habits of the client be assessed to determine whether the assigned material has been perused or *not used at all!* The importance of his study must be driven home or else he will expect the counselor to provide all input and actually work his problem *for* him. This is especially true of a person who has spent many hours in therapy; he frequently expects the doctor to "do it to him" while he is passive in the whole process. He must be "advised of his rights" by the counselor in that his progress is going to be directly proportionate to the time spent in the assigned study of the Word and supplementary materials under the tutelage of the Therapist, the Holy Spirit. If he protests that he hasn't time for study, then it might be well to suggest that he is too busy for counseling until he can arrange time for the necessary study. Once the above determinations have been made, the counselor should be pretty well apprised of the spiritual temperature of the client so that he can proceed to build upon the spiritual foundation and framework laid in the first interview.

If time permits at the end of the second hour, it is helpful to present appropriate diagrams to give the client a thorough understanding of the interactions between soul and spirit, particularly the function of the will. Most persons are conditioned by past experience to believe (with the mind) that the emotions must concur with the choice made by the will or a valid decision has not been made. When it becomes abundantly clear to the client that he is not responsible to *change* his life but only to *select the power source,* a great stride has been taken.

The power source for living the Christian life or walking in the Spirit is the Holy Spirit, who indwells each believer; the opposing force which energizes the flesh is the power of indwelling sin. There is no neutral ground; the personality or soul is influenced by one power or the other in making moral choices. Satan, the enemy of souls, is the author of indwelling sin and delights in his master art of deception. He would much rather have us be good (humanistically speaking), moral, and even involved in the work of the Church as Christians than to be involved in something we know to be sin. In the latter case, it would eventually be recognized as such under the conviction of the Spirit and would be dealt with to the detriment of Satan's cause. He blinds the eyes of sinners to the gospel, but *he also blinds the eyes of Christians to their resources in Christ.*

The person who has entered counseling has found some situation with which he is unable to cope. He usually does not realize that he has the option to confront the situation and life as a whole in the energizing power of the Spirit rather than gritting his teeth, doing his best, and expecting God to *help* him. When we pray a "help me" prayer it might be well to analyze what we are saying. A person who hires a helper in some occupation or profession usually does not expect the helper to take the load in performing the work. The skilled artisan will perform; the helper will do just that—*help*. When we ask the Lord to help us in this or that, we are tacitly saying, "*I* will do the work; but, Lord, I need Your help here and there!" It will be the Christian doing the work with His help or it will be "not I, but Christ" (Galatians 2:20).

The function of the will is again the key factor; by faith (an act of obedience of the will) we walk in the Spirit (Galatians 5:16), or by default (if not volitionally) we will walk *after* the flesh. A person may undergo behavior modification by his parents or a therapist or rigidly discipline himself and thereby do a passable job of keeping the law in *man's* sight, but in the sight of God it adds up to self-righteousness at best. If he does a superlative job of training the flesh to serve the Lord, doing the *do's* and avoiding the *taboos,* there may be considerable pride involved—and God has some rather specific things to say about pride!

When the big picture is clearly understood, the client sees that it is not his symptoms which are of utmost importance, nor is the resolution of his particular situation; but it is of paramount importance as to who is getting the glory out of his living—himself or the Lord. Decisive dealing with this issue may well be the turning point as the person is faced with all of the implications of the cross and is willing to submerge his interests to the greater cause of Christ.

The battle lines are now clearly drawn between the Spirit of God and the power of sin, with the objective being the control of the mind of the client. The counselor is God's representative to the client to aid him in sorting out the deceptive advances and decoys presented by indwelling sin which would prevent him from understanding and accepting truth. As God's representative, the counselor is to manifest the love of Christ to the client while faithfully opening up the truth of God's Word and exposing the offerings and deceptions of the power of sin as the Enemy mounts his counterattack. The presentation of truth takes two forms: giving the client objective understanding about himself as he relates to himself and others, and giving him an understanding of God and his relationship to Him through his position in Christ.

The Word says we should speak the truth in love (Ephesians 4:15). This principle is cardinal in such a counseling relationship, since the client must know that he is loved and accepted by the counselor for the counselor to be able to say what must be said. To many, the counselor's love and acceptance may be the first the client has ever experienced; others have known acceptance when their performance was up to par but are convinced that no one can accept them after knowing their innermost heart of hearts and the behavior which has emanated from it.

Thus, the counseling path takes two prongs: (1) the client's increased understanding of himself and how his *past* influences his *present* and (2) the client's understanding of his relationship to God and how he can appropriate all that Christ *is* for all that he *needs*.

Self-understanding

Most of the damaged emotions which result in distorting reality or taking flights from reality may be explained to the satisfaction of the client in terms of rejection. To do so, the counselor must have thoroughly understood his own past rejection patterns and/or studied the rejection syndrome to the point where he can readily pick up the thread of rejection in a client's life and aid him in understanding the fabric woven from it. As in most fabrics, the surface may look beautiful but the underside may be tangled, snarled, and knotted. It is not necessary to unravel all of this, but it can be very helpful to understand what caused it and the problems it causes for those who come in contact with it.

Since the rejection syndrome operates in a unique manner within each individual and causes him to have a particular pattern of relating to others, it is impossible to set down a formula for detection and explanation which may be utilized routinely. Rather, the counselor must rely on the Counselor to give him insight that he, in turn, might explain it to the client. Usually, it is so apparent that the client will pick it up and begin to relate to the counselor the many ways that he is rejecting others and destroying relationships although he had never realized it until he was given the key for understanding himself. Understanding of these basics is sufficient, since this is merely the manner in which the flesh functions (or malfunctions) in the particular individual.

To assist the counselor in recognizing the rejection syndrome, the following clues to recognition of overt and covert rejection are given. They will alert the counselor when he hears them in the counseling interview.

Clues in Identifying Rejection

Those to whom rejection is an unfamilar concept as the progenitor of emotional disturbances may find it difficult to ferret it out in the more subtle forms. Likewise, the person who is fortunate enough to have experienced little rejection in his formative years will find it more difficult to identify and also more difficult to identify with the individual troubled by it.

The following situations and statements will help the counselor to recognize the rejection syndrome.

Examples of Overt Rejection

1. *Rejective statements* such as:
   (a) "I wish you had never been born!"
   (b) "I do not love you!"
   (c) "You will never amount to anything!"
   (d) "You are just like your father (or mother)!"
2. *Physical violence and battering.*
3. *Sexual molestation by parent.* The body is accepted but the person is rejected.
4. *Being given up for adoption by relatives or others.* The damage is accentuated when other siblings remain with the natural parents.
5. *Being ejected from the home.* Example: An adolescent came home one evening after a hard day's work to find the doors and windows locked. As a result, he was forced to find a place to work for his room and board to complete high school. This trauma was added to that of seeing his mother taken to a mental institution in his preteen years, which resulted in teasing by his peers.
6. *Ill treatment by stepparent.* The presence of a stepparent should always be examined to determine whether a rejective environment existed (or exists).
7. *Encouragement of sinful or antisocial behavior by parent.* Example: Occasionally one runs across a male who has been taken to a house of prostitution by his father to initiate him in sexual activity and teach him the "ways of a man."
8. *Being forced into adult responsibilities before adulthood.* Example: One man had been forced by his father to earn his own way at age thirteen. In turn, he had several children who received the same treatment upon entering their teen years.

Examples of Covert or Subtle Rejection

1. *Premature death of parents.* Although the parent may have had no choice, the child has lost the benefit of the parent's presence. In such a case it is well to determine if the remaining parent remarried—and, if so, the child's age at the time and his circumstances in the intervening time. With whom did he live? How was he treated? Does he remember the death? How does he relate to the sex of the parent who died?

2. *Broken home.* A divorce invariably results in rejection of the children by one or both parents. The events leading up to the divorce are usually traumatic as well. The aftermath necessarily means that one parent is absent, so it behooves the counselor to see how each parent subsequently related to the child.

3. *Conditional love.* The child who always had to "measure up" to win parental approval could gain acceptance only of his performance, not his *person.* Therefore, *he* could be rejected while his *performance* was being accepted.

4. *Change-of-life baby.* Inquiring about the age of the mother when the person was born can be very revealing. Comparatively few parents plan children after age forty. Some such children are openly told they were an accident or a tagalong.

5. *Wrong sex.* A person can get the message from his parent(s) that a child of the opposite sex was desired. A girl might become a tomboy in order to gain her father's approval in such a case. If she is successful, her *performance* as a boy is accepted but her *person* as a female isn't.

6. *Preferential treatment of a sibling.* Favoritism shown other children can result in great harm. Some parents are very open in naming their favorites. Example: An affluent family had two sons who were talented and mentally gifted. The older was both

overprotected and indulged with material things. He had only to think of an extravagant item for a birthday and it was his. His brother (two years younger) might, by contrast, become the proud possessor of a cheap camera! The older was under psychiatric treatment but he reported that the younger was in much worse condition than he! Both had been soundly rejected, with the parents probably being unaware of it.

7. *The only child.* It is not infrequent that an only child is overprotected and/or indulged, since there are *two* parents to do and decide for *one* child. "Smothering" may also be a problem.

8. *Younger sibling.* The youngest in the family is frequently accorded different treatment from that of his predecessors. If his elders have gone astray, the parents may clamp down on him. Or, they may recognize their error in being too hard on the older ones and become too lenient with him. Most have heard of new parents who dutifully sterilize everything that goes into baby's mouth. Thus, when he drops his pacifier, it must be sterilized before he gets it back. With the second child, the pacifier would be picked up, wiped off and reinserted. And the third child might receive the pacifier directly from the floor into his mouth!

9. *Eldest child.* The eldest may well be the victim of unrealistic expectations and be pushed to excel beyond his ability and/or motivation; the parent(s) reputation may hinge on the child's success, with the child being well aware of his responsibility to produce.

10. *Adoption.* The child who has been adopted has, by definition, been rejected. Otherwise, he would yet be with his natural parents. The age and circumstances under which he lost his parents may serve to mitigate or amplify the resulting trauma to his emotional makeup. Sooner or later the child will experience an identity problem, since he doesn't know the parents with whom he should be able to identify. This can

result in a lifelong search unless he learns early to establish his identity in Christ.

11. *Prolonged childhood illness.* Such an illness can result in overprotection by the parents which may continue after the illness has long been cured. The inordinate amount of attention necessitated by the illness may result in one or more of the other siblings receiving less than their fair share of the parent's time.

12. *Hospitalization at an early age.* A prolonged stay in a hospital, where it is impossible for the parents to love the child appropriately, may result in a perceived rejection. This is especially damaging in the early months of life when the need to be held and fondled is the greatest. Also, the emotional damage sustained cannot be rationalized at the time, nor can the circumstances be recalled later.

13. *Absentee parent.* A parent may be forced to spend protracted periods of time away from the family because of his employment. Unavoidable though this may be, the child or children do not have access to the time or the love which the parent may have for them in abundance. Shift work, too, may prevent the phasing of schedules which would allow effective time together.

14. *Invidious comparison with sibling(s).* At times, parents hold up the record of an older sibling for those following to hit or miss. In other cases one sibling may compare himself with another and reject himself without the aid of the parents. Teachers may unwittingly compare younger children with those who have gone before, and those who are less gifted may find it impossible to make the mark.

15. *Handicapped or flawed child.* Children with a pronounced defect may be the butt of jokes on the school ground, or even subjected to criticism or ridicule by their parents. The resulting emotional damage may be carried for a lifetime. Inordinate medical expenses

may bankrupt the parents, and the child may feel responsible for it.

16. *Undemonstrative parents.*   Parents may be able to express love in words but unable to show it by embracing, etc. Or, the opposite may be the case, where the parents show love by doing but cannot verbalize it.

17. *Boarding away from home.*   At times circumstances make it impossible for the child to live at home, as may be the case with the children of missionaries. The parents may have both the desire and ability to verbalize and show love but may be denied the opportunity. A small child finds it impossible not to perceive rejection in such cases.

18. *Being "seen but not heard."*   Some children get the message that they will deserve the right to be a person and express themselves after they grow up, only to find in adulthood that they have never learned how.

19. *Punishment to vent parental hostility.*   When punishment is used more to rid the parent of his frustration than to cleanse the child's conscience, the child has experienced rejection.

20. *Overprotection.*   Many of the foregoing involve varying degrees of limiting the child's right to be a person. Extreme cases are obvious, but the more subtle behaviors may not be as easily discerned.

Summary

The foregoing, rightly understood, will give the counselor a repertoire of rejective behaviors and attitudes for which to look that will serve him well as he endeavors to understand neurotic (or psychotic) behavior. He will then be equipped to interpret cause and effect to the client prior to giving him a clear understanding of his acceptance in Christ.

To further exemplify the rejection syndrome in an individual and in the extended family, the following account is given and pictorially presented in Diagram 7.

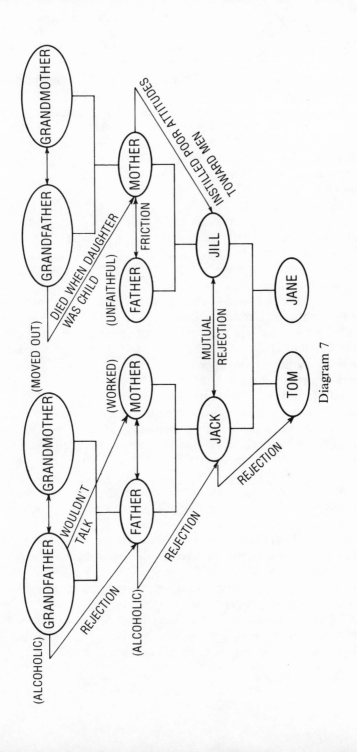

Diagram 7

Jack and Jill had gone to a pastor for counseling and had been unable to resolve long-standing difficulties. She had asked her husband to leave the house after more than ten years of marriage because she could no longer tolerate his rejection of their son, Tom. As illustrated, they also had a daughter, Jane, whom he had no trouble loving. He could give no rational explanation as to why he rejected Tom, who was a good-looking, outgoing child. He made no attempt to deny the rejection and was eager for help. Jack was extremely shy and found it impossible to talk in family gatherings. Jill had accused him of infidelity almost from the honeymoon on account of her own insecurity. As the history was taken in the individual interviews, several rejection patterns became obvious, with one pattern impinging upon the other.

Jack had been told in a subtle way that he was unwanted; he was an only child, which underscored the point. His father was an alcoholic and his mother worked. His grandfather and grandmother also lived in the home, and the grandfather too was alcoholic. Grandfather isolated himself, so she, Grandmother, got the idea that she wasn't wanted and moved out.

Jill's father was unfaithful to her mother and eventually married the other woman. Prior to the divorce there was continual friction between them. Jill's maternal grandfather died when her mother was a child. Jill's mother never remarried and was not pleased when her daughter related to her father and his new wife.

Now that the stage is set, let's look at the rejection involved in this narrative. The counselor asked Jack how many men he had greatly respected in his lifetime; he could not name *one!* It was pointed out to him that his alcoholic father and grandfather had been poor examples of men, and he knew that he, a male, had been unwanted. Being disillusioned with and rejected by the male sex, he proceeded to reject himself and his son, who also had the misfortune of being male!

Jill had witnessed her father's rejection of her mother and the family to go with another woman. This was the second rejection by a man experienced by her mother since her father had died and left her when she was a small child. Thus, Mother never remarried, which insured that no other man would have the opportunity to get close enough to hurt her again through loving her and leaving her. Jill grew up with the feeling that men were not to be trusted and probably had some reminders by her mother now and then.

The marriage began with her accusations of infidelity, which did little to build Jack's confidence in himself. The one point upon which they thoroughly agreed was that men were no good! Neither had recognized the foregoing rejection or the impact which it had on their individual lives and their marriage. Both came to understand it in the first individual interview and appropriated Christ as life. The changes wrought in their lives by the Holy Spirit resulted in their being back together by the end of the first week of counseling.

Their son, Tom, received some counseling, and Jack was soon able to show him love and acceptance because of his own newfound identity in Christ. Also, Jack was now able to cease rejecting his wife and let her get close to him, since in Christ, he was safe. She had died to her own insecurity and was now free to trust him and submit to his headship in Christ.

Very shortly, the entire family had united with a Bible-teaching church and were involving others in Bible study to share the identification truths. Rejection had been replaced with acceptance in Christ.

Although the focus of counseling may return to self-understanding from time to time, attention should now be turned to a more complete understanding of what it means to be identified with Christ in death, burial, resurrection, and being seated at the right hand of God.

Understanding of Position in Christ

As with self-understanding, there is no one approach which is a panacea to opening up a person's understanding of his identity in Christ. With one the Holy Spirit illuminates one portion of the Word, and with another it may be completely different. The use of diagrams to depict scriptural truths has been found to be vital in unlocking Truth to clients. The Wheel and Line and other diagrams contained herein will serve as a starting place for those who see diagrams as something helpful. With most counselors it is found that they are not comfortable with diagrams developed by someone else and must make modifications or else develop their own. This is as it should be, since what we use must first have been processed through us before it will ever have meaning for others.

The interview will consist of probing and sharing as led of the Spirit until the client has a clear intellectual understanding of what Christ has done for him and who he is in Christ. Once the understanding of underlying psychological symptoms is gained, interpersonal problems understood, and the scriptural answer is understood (if not applied), the order of business is to see if there are impediments to appropriating resources in Christ.

Appropriation of Christ as Life

There are those unique individuals who can appropriate Christ as life as soon as they are shown the answer under the leading of the Holy Spirit. For every one who can simply in faith and obedience claim his answer in Christ, there are several who seemingly must struggle and grapple with every truth they hear. After all of the truth has been explained and it seems there is no more teaching that can be done, *this* is where the true work of the spiritual guide begins. The Holy Spirit must give unique guidance for each case, that the counselor may help the client see what might be preventing his appropriating the victory which has already been won.

The basic problem here is to discern the obstacles or hindrances faced by the client which prevent his moving on into victory. These are discussed beginning on page 52 of chapter 4, and the counselor should be prayerfully trusting the Holy Spirit to point out to him and the client what the holdup is. In many cases, merely identifying it is sufficient for the client to deal with it and claim victory by faith. Usually the client must "see" what he is doing (or not doing) before he can "see" by illumination of the Holy Spirit what God is ready and able to do about it.

Occasional clients will go for several interviews with no apparent change at all, while some will have an increase in symptoms and get worse! It is in such cases that the faith of the counselor is tested: Will he hang in there and trust God, or give up in defeat? It is not infrequent that the faith of the client is directly hinged to the faith of the counselor. It is not unscriptural for the client to believe God's *work* in the counselor when he finds it next to impossible to rely totally on God's *Word* (John 14:11).

There are times when the counselor is on the brink of giving up hope that the client is *ever* going to change, and then the Spirit of God begins to move in a mighty way. The counselor must ever be kept mindful that it is not *his* work but *His* work that is going to get the job done!

7

Uppers and Downers

The ultimate goal of the counselor is to see his client break into victory over the power of indwelling sin and the enslavement to past patterns of thinking, feeling, and acting. The way in which this is revealed to the individual by the Holy Spirit is unique to his case, and the ways in which believers handle victory are just as varied. Again, there are many parallels to the salvation experience. Some have emotional releases as the result of the regenerating work of the Holy Spirit; others do not. Some have radical changes in behavior immediately upon conversion; others have a more gradual transition. Some are influenced greatly by their emotions in the early days of their Christian experience; others seem to be anchored in the Word with its objectivity almost from the beginning. Some are consistent in their Christian walk; others are quite erratic. On and on could go the differences found in new believers, and the same type of comparisons may be made with those who appropriate Christ as life. Just as there are differing responses upon entering into His victory, there are also varied patterns in the period immediately following.

It is not the counselor's responsibility to dictate to the client how he should act or react in Christ but to admonish him relative to some of the perils ahead. There are those who have a "high" or a near euphoria upon release from the shackles of the self-life that held them in bondage. This is not to be challenged or put down, but the individual must know that the euphoric condition *can not* and *will not* be a way of life. Some would live on the mountaintop continuously and begin to seek experiences which will give them another fix to maintain the high. It is herein that the problem lies; they would walk by *feelings*—not by *faith*. Such kicks pander to the self-life, and the novice may find himself getting a fix from the power of indwelling sin while attributing it to the Holy Spirit. Those who have been extremely neurotic have sufficient reason to enjoy "good" feelings for a change and are loathe to let go of this initial period of *feeling,* as well as *knowing,* the Lord's nearness. Many are the substitutes for solid spiritual growth which will undoubtedly be brought across the path of the believer who is young in the Christ-life. Counterfeits are available for anything God has to offer. The believer who depends on feelings, "highs," and experiences has a long way to fall from his "high"—and fall he will, unless he has benefit of proper counsel to see how he can "level out" as he walks in the light of objective Truth. Since the "lows" are as extreme as the "highs," there will frequently be deep depression, to the point of doubting salvation or recurrent thoughts of suicide.

The astute reader will discern that there is every bit as much danger, if not more, in the highs as there is in the lows. The person who is able to find a means of supporting the highs is very likely to get hooked on it and begin pushing it as the panacea for the needs of everyone. The person on a low is highly unlikely to evangelize that particular viewpoint; if he did, he would find few takers, since most folks have all the misery they can handle already.

The mood swings described above are bound to come to all in some degree; as we walk in the Spirit we are *up,* and as we walk after the flesh, we are *down.* The problem lies in pressing the "up" to make it a "high," or in capitulating to the "low" and following it all the way to the bottom. Both are indicative of *a passive will which allows experience to follow hard on the heels of emotion.*

The client must be forewarned to lock in on objective Truth, the Word of God, and ignore emotions, whether good or bad, as an indication of God's working or leading. As he *begins* this

way and *proceeds* this way, he can praise the Lord when he
senses the Lord's closeness at those special times—but he can
also praise the Lord when sense data fails to confirm the
Lord's presence at all!

Such instruction may be given to the newly victorious Christian, but it seems as though he has a leaky head (or heart).
Despite all warnings to the contrary, the newfound victory,
when based on confirmation by his emotions, proves to be a
fleeting one. When he returns for counseling to see what happened, he is usually singing the woe-is-me blues in harmony
with the Tempter, who would have him believe that all is lost,
never to be regained.

The counselor's role is to point him back to objective truth
and away from subjective experience. As he does this it is
necessary to help him analyze his situation and see where he
got off track. Usually it will be discovered that he settled back
to enjoy victory and was lulled into passivity by the power of
indwelling sin which subsequently energized his personality
and fostered the flesh condition once more. In such a condition
he will respond to adverse circumstances, such as rejection, in
a similar manner as before—*and* reap the same benefits.

A case in point is a lady who suffered severe depression for
forty years and had suffered many things of many physicians,
including a broken back as a result of electroconvulsive
therapy. The years and years and years of therapy of various
kinds had served to break *her* back but it hadn't broken the
back of the haunting depression. Upon realizing the genesis of
her symptoms (her mother had told her from birth that she was
unwanted), she appropriated Christ as life, and the depression
lifted almost immediately. Victory was sweet for a few days,
even though she was in a nursing home at age seventy-two
while recovering from a broken hip. The counselor dropped in
to see her to find her running a "pity party" again, with depression as per usual.

The counselor helped her to retrace her steps from victory
into depression that she might again clearly see the way out.
The first question was: "What caused the depression initially?"

The reply was: "Rejection by my mother." The next question was: "What happened today that was out of the ordinary?" As she thought over the day, she recalled two major events:

(1) Her sister had dropped by to tell her good-bye and was departing for an extended trip.
(2) Her daughter-in-law came by with a grandson who was leaving for another state.

She was then asked how she reacted to their leaving and she saw immediately that their leaving her alone in the nursing home had been perceived as another rejection. She had reacted as before and had thrown an internal temper tantrum, otherwise known as depression. Once she saw the sequence of events and recognized her reaction, she smiled and gladly yielded again to the Lord—and let Him meet this new need and return her to victory.

Downers are always handled in pretty much the same manner, but victory doesn't always return immediately. It seems that God allows us to walk on the bottom for some protracted time to teach us to walk by faith. When we are content to walk by faith whether we are up, down, or in between, we will gradually or suddenly return to a spiritual equilibrium.

One other pitfall which is worthy of mention is the spiritual warfare which confronts the believer who appropriates Christ as life. Since Christ now has the ascendancy in the life, and with it the freedom to live and work through him, he is also promoted to the front lines of combat. Upon finding himself at the front lines, it is not at all surprising that the Enemy begins to take some potshots at him. This is an altogether new arena for most Christians. It seems that just as soon as they have subdued the enemy within they become the target of the Enemy from without. The victory has been won with the Enemy vanquished, but he will be unrelenting in his attempts to thwart the believer's resolve of ". . . having done all, to stand" (Ephesians 6:13).

The counselor's function, as always, is to remind the embattled believer of his victory in the Victor and then to stand with him against the Enemy. Although the counselor may stand with him and resist the Enemy with him, it is ultimately each believer to whom James 4:7 is addressed. It is not that we should have someone resist for us but that we might stand (Ephesians 6:10–18) and resist (James 4:7) and see the Enemy flee. There is some truth mixed with much error in some present-day approaches to dealing with the devil. Many have declared all-out warfare and are on the offensive in actively chasing the devil. This all sounds very courageous on the surface, but the Bible says to stand, resist, and the devil will flee! How much energy we could save ourselves if we stood in the power of the Spirit and let the *devil* do the running!

Many of those who deal with the devil by casting out demons are at best dealing with spiritual symptoms, much as the psychiatrist or psychologist deals with psychological symptoms. Unless the source, the flesh, is cut off through the operation of the Cross in blocking the power of indwelling sin, the person has not really been done a favor. The flesh is a cauldron from which emanate many deceptive guises. To deal with the product *without dealing with the source* is but to invite disaster. To admit the source and to deny the possibility of its utilization by its author would be foolhardy, to say the least.

The counselor is initially and continually to aid the client in putting an end to the tyranny of the flesh and to walk consistently in the Spirit by abiding where he has been placed—*in Christ*. Learning to deal with uppers and downers should be a progressive learning experience. Initially, the newly victorious Christian will learn how to deal with the downer after he is in the midst of it. The secret to maintaining victory is to become spiritually discerning that the attitude which predisposes the individual to yield to indwelling sin may be dealt with in its incipient stages; in other words, deal with the attitude in the power of the Spirit before the *act* becomes a *fact!*

Continually reckoning upon death to the power of indwelling sin (Romans 6:11) and yielding the members as instruments of righteousness (Romans 6:13) will result in continual victory. Preventive reckoning will obviate remedial reckoning! Resurgence of defeatist attitudes is a precursor to carnal thoughts and actions.

"But if we walk in the light, as he is in the light, we have fellowship one with another, and the blood of Jesus Christ his Son cleanseth us from all sin" (1 John 1:7).

8

The Bible in Spirituotherapy

Minister the Word

Up to this point very little has been said concerning the use of Scripture in counseling. It will be noted in the following narrative that a significant departure from some conventional applications of the Word of God is advocated. This is not to say that it is incorrect to use the Word as some suggest; but, too frequently, it is used in the manner of a Band-Aid, dealing with symptoms, when it is more than sufficient for the problem as well!

A method of using Scripture to deal with symptoms which is commonly accepted may be found in a host of books or booklets on personal work. Some have alphabetical listings of symptoms, such as fear, worry, depression, etc. One can turn to his particular symptom (take fear, for instance) and find passages such as Isaiah 41:10: "Fear thou not; for I am with thee: be not dismayed; for I am thy God: I will strengthen thee; yea, I will help thee; yea, I will uphold thee with the right hand of my righteousness." Or another favorite—2 Timothy 1:7: "For God hath not given us the spirit of fear; but of power, and of love, and of a sound mind."

These two verses meant much to me during my search for an answer to the plaguing worries, doubts, and fears which were my lot for years. God, in His mercy, gave me many such verses as I fought my *symptoms,* while He was progressively weakening me to lead me to understand the *problem* so He could become my answer. During the past years of counseling, hundreds of persons have reported the same pattern. Many pastors have been trained to use the Scriptures in this manner. It is not *wrong,* but it is not *sufficient!* When the *product* of the flesh such as fear is mistaken for the problem, verses as wonderful and comforting as the two quoted above can well become a palliative to soothe the flesh. When the flesh is taught to use Scripture for its own comfort, the end result differs little from therapy, which is also comforting to the flesh. This is not to deprecate the Scripture in any way, but rather to elevate it to the lofty position it should and must have—being used as God intended it.

Another such use of Scripture is quoting it to replace unwanted and/or sinful thoughts. On the surface this sounds like the thing to do, and there is certainly great benefit in memorizing and meditating upon the Word of God. However, a person with self or flesh in the ascendancy can use Scripture to replace thoughts, thereby dealing with the symptoms (the thoughts) and strengthening self in the process! A moment's reflection would cause a person to see that thoughts could also be replaced by quoting the Constitution. The Scripture, of course, has the advantage in that it may later be applied by the Holy Spirit to deal wih the problem as well as the symptoms.

Yet another very common variation of the use of Scripture, almost tantamount to escape reading, is to spend so much time studying history and prophecy that discipleship is all but forgotten. Let me hasten to emphasize that there is great benefit in knowing Old Testament history and profiting by the experiences of the Old Testament saints, along with claiming its many promises. Likewise, there is much to be said for understanding prophecy concerning the end times which are upon us. Sad to say, there are so many who study prophecy and live for the blessed hope of Titus 2:13 because they are not aware of any hope for victory here on earth. Such Christians can frequently debate with fervor (if not hostility) the positions—or at least their own position—on the Tribulation, to the point of breaking fellowship with other believers or splitting a church or fellowship of churches.

When the whole counsel of God is not taught, the portion of truth that is taught may be emphasized to the point where error creeps in. When history, prophecy, and evangelism are taught at the expense of discipleship or spiritual growth, the result can be an increase in knowledge without sufficient life and wisdom to maintain balance and utilize the knowledge to God's glory.

The Great Commission is warrant enough that evangelism should be a central focus in the Church and in the life of the believer; however, to stop with using the Word for evangelism is to teach birth without sufficient spiritual nutrition for growth. There are pastors without number who will take almost any passage in the Word and use it as a jumping-off place for an evangelistic message. History is meaningless unless we connect it to the gospel; prophecy is a warning to get ready; or, if already reborn, prophecy should spur us on to winning others while there is yet time—and so it goes—and, all too frequently, it stops right there! Again, this use of the Word is right and commendable, but Christians who are limited to such a diet are stunted in their growth to the point where many leave the Church nursing the same neuroses with which they entered it. Such persons are unable to produce because of crippling emotional hang-ups, and the inability to produce creates further anxiety which eventually forces them to look elsewhere for an answer. When this has been their lot in a fundamental church, they may seek an answer outside the Church—and their "progress" is rapidly downhill.

None of the foregoing uses of the Word is wrong, and none is to be discouraged; but would that the person who ministers the Word *of* God might simultaneously minister the Word who *is* God! Hebrews 1:1, 2 states: "God . . . hath in these last days spoken unto us by his Son . . . ." The written Word should be a vehicle for ministering the Living Word in the power of the Holy Spirit.

The Bible *is* a book of history, a book of prophecy, a book of promises to help in time of need, and *the* book on soul-winning; but it is so much more than that: It is the Book of *Life!* Its promises go beyond new birth and forgiveness of sins to life in ". . . him that is able to do exceeding abundantly above all that we ask or think, according to the *power that worketh in us*" (Ephesians 3:20, *italics added*).

Now that we have digressed and covered some approaches to using the Scriptures which fall short of teaching Christ as life, let's proceed to lay down some overall parameters for utilizing the Scriptures in teaching spiritual growth or discipleship. At the end of the chapter are listed some of the passages which have been found to be meaningful to many as the truths of identification with Christ began to grip them.

It is not the author's intent to provide an arsenal of Scripture with explicit instructions as to which to fire and the firing order. It is assumed that the Christian who would attempt to use the information outlined herein has hidden sufficient passages of Scripture in his heart that the Spirit of God may call them forth.

As alluded to above, the use of Scriptures can be described in military parlance. The *rifle* approach of taking a specific Scripture to meet a specific need as directed by the Holy Spirit can be life transforming.

The *shotgun* approach of shooting at the crowd and hoping to hit someone is less efficient but necessary when dealing with groups; not everyone will get all that he needs, but the Holy Spirit can tailor a message so that everyone gets something.

The *artillery* approach would more aptly describe the use of Scripture in counseling, since it is desired to fire a "pattern" which will encompass the teaching of the growth truths. Once the pattern has been laid out, it is necessary to isolate the "pockets of resistance" and deal with them with weapons (Scriptures) suitable for the task at hand. These pockets of resistance were described as obstacles or hindrances to appropriating Christ as life in chapter 4.

The ground is charted for the application of the patterns through the use of diagrams previously learned, or developed spontaneously, under the leadership of the Spirit. The "Supreme Commander" knows the enemy (flesh), the arsenal (the Word of God), and the strategy (cutting off the supply line to the flesh—the power of indwelling sin), and the precise timing required to engineer the demise of self and occupy the enemy-held territory!

The counselor cannot fight the client's battles for him, nor is this his purpose; since he has previously been led of the Spirit in negotiating the hostile terrain, he can not only map the path but can lead his client to appropriate the victory which has already been won.

The Enemy

In any military situation it is vital to know the enemy, his whereabouts, his campaign strategy, to be able to decode his messages and see through his camouflage. The diagrams and supporting Scriptures have as their first goal exposing the flesh or self that the client may see through the ruses (symptoms) and camouflage (self-righteousness, good works, etc.) used by the power of sin to fake him out. Almost all clients enter counseling viewing the symptoms ("mental illness," marital difficulties, problems with children, etc.) as the problems. Many are sincere in believing that smoking, alcoholism, emotional disturbances, etc., are the problems, and self has been vainly struggling to cut off some of its own tentacles with varying degrees of "success" and "failure." The discouraging thing is that, like some organisms, it merely grows replacement tentacles! They might perchance have a different shape but *always* the same disgusting *source!* Therefore, it is of utmost importance to expose the source through the use of diagrams and Scriptures that the attack might be directed at the heart of the enemy's strength!

Once the enemy has been dislodged from his hiding place and is out in the open it is a simple matter to annihilate him if the proper weapons are available. The same Scriptures that exposed the enemy also reveal the one and only weapon—the Cross (Galatians 2:20; Romans 6:6, 11, 13), but the flesh will go to any extreme to avoid it. *Christians will work themselves to death for the Lord to avoid appropriating by simple faith their death with Him!* They will go to any length to attempt self-

improvement in an effort to avoid self-*abasement*. Only when the Spirit of God has used circumstances and the Scriptures to strip off the camouflage and expose self for the vile thing it is, is the person prepared for the weapon (the Cross) to do its work.

As in any war, the victory is only as secure as the peace that is maintained. Though the enemy (the flesh) is vanquished, it is not incapable of regrouping and rebuilding its strength to do battle once again (Galatians 5:17). The source of supply (power of indwelling sin) is blocked initially (Romans 6:11) and continually (2 Corinthians 4:11; Luke 9:23) by the Cross. To state Galatians 5:16 in the *converse:* "If you do not walk in the Spirit, you *will* fulfill the lust of the flesh."

Keeping the peace is equally important to winning the war. Deceptions here can be very subtle as the enemy seeks to throw up camouflage in order to get into operation again. Sometimes the flesh does battle *against* Christ (Galatians 3:3), and at other times it works assiduously *for* Him; but in either case it is still *battling,* which demonstrates it has again connected with its source of supply.

A continuous reckoning (or counting) on the operation of the Cross in the life (Romans 6:11) is vital to continued victory. If the flesh is permitted to function again, not only does the enemy throw more flak but its old ally and sponsor, Satan, may provide some reinforcements (seeking whom he may devour) in an attempt to regain lost ground. As the Christian is loosed from the shackles of the enemy, he will be able to point others to the same victory and show them the way through (the Cross). When the Christian is adept at detecting and bringing to naught the enemy within, the Enemy without, Satan, must employ more grandiose tactics, such as oppression. If he can't disable from within, he will try to contain with his big net from without!

The Christian "in the net," so to speak, has need not only of counsel to help him recognize the net but also of the support of those not so entangled who can pray that the Spirit of God will cut the net. However, the majority of the Christians "without" are still so busily engaged fighting their own civil war (with the flesh) while having some skirmishes with principalities and powers (Ephesians 6) that they are all but helpless to participate in rescuing the hapless victim.

Once the Christian has learned the art of warfare with the Enemy from without and has learned to "stand" (Ephesians 6:10–14) rather than be routed or entangled in the net of the Enemy, he is able to lead others to the Cross to appropriate victory. Also, he is enabled by the control of the Holy Spirit to wield the sword of the Spirit (the Word of God) in slicing through the net of oppression and freeing those held captive.

Maintenance of victory means that the supply lines must be kept open to the peacekeeping force. During this time it must be remembered that we fight from a standpoint *of* victory, not to *attain* victory. The enemy (flesh) will be certain to try to infiltrate the ranks. Taking our position (in Christ) and standing against the enemy within and the Enemy without in resurrection life, our supply lines are to be the Word of God, prayer, fellowship with victorious believers as all are anointed by the Spirit of God.

Once we have appropriated our victory over sin on planet Earth, we will not be looking for the "blessed hope" as a cop-out; but constantly abiding in our victorious Victor, we will welcome Him as He returns as a blessed and eternal cop-*in!*

Assignments

Portions of the Word should be assigned for study prior to the next interview, consistent with the discerned need. For the unsaved, it will be a concentrated study, preferably with a study guide, of the way of salvation—principally in the books of John and Romans. For the Christian, the study should focus primarily on Romans 6, 7, and 8, Galatians, Ephesians, Philippians, and Colossians.

It has been helpful to many to read Romans 6, 7, and 8 the first day, then Galatians, Ephesians, Philippians, and Colossians each in its turn. As the portion is read, it is suggested that the reader pause and reflect upon the mention of "in Christ," "in Him," "in whom," or references to our identification with Him in death, burial, resurrection, ascension, and seating in the heavenlies. The Holy Spirit is trusted to direct in the study as well as to illuminate that which is studied.

Suggested Scriptures for
Meditation During Counseling

The following passages are a mere drop in the bucket but should serve to stimulate the reader to have available for recall Scriptures which both guide and comfort those with whom he would serve as a spiritual guide. Those which will enjoy God's blessing will usually be passages which have had the most meaning in the reader's spiritual journey; he may point another with confidence to those promises which have been fulfilled in his own life.

The "plan of identification" is most succinctly stated in Romans 6:6 (know); Romans 6:11 (reckon, or count upon); and Romans 6:13 (yield).

The truth that we must become weak before He can be strong within us is the theme of the following:

2 Corinthians 12:9, 10
2 Corinthians 13:4
2 Corinthians 4:7–12
2 Chronicles 26:5, 16
Psalm 142

The necessity and blessing of suffering:

Philippians 1:29, 30
Isaiah 43:2
Isaiah 48:10
Isaiah 54:7, 8
1 Peter 2:20, 21
1 Peter 5:10
1 Peter 1:6, 7

1 Peter 4:12–14
2 Timothy 2:11–13
Philippians 3:7–10

God's faithfulness:

1 Corinthians 10:13
2 Timothy 2:13 (read several versions)
2 Thessalonians 3:3
1 Thessalonians 5:24

The Christian's resources:

Ephesians 1:3, 19, 20
Colossians 2:9, 10
Ephesians 3:16–20
Colossians 1:9–11, 27
Colossians 3:1–4

The Christian's responsibility:

I beseech you therefore, brethren, by the mercies of God, that ye present your bodies a living sacrifice, holy, acceptable unto God, which is *your* reasonable service.

Romans 12:1 (*italics added*)

The Christian's expectations:

And be not conformed to this world: *but be ye transformed by the renewing of your mind* [God's part], that ye may prove what is that good, and acceptable, and perfect, will of God.

Romans 12:2 (*italics added*)

And we know that all things work together for good to them that love God, to them who are the called according to his purpose. For whom he did foreknow, he also did predestinate *to be conformed to the image of his Son,* that he might be the firstborn among many brethren.

Romans 8:28, 29 (*italics added*)

Since it is God's ultimate purpose to make us like His Son, the Lord Jesus Christ, it should come as no surprise to us that this process should entail suffering. We are certainly no better than our Lord, who endured suffering to purchase our salvation on that instrument of death, the cross. As that instrument of death is applied to the self-life by the Holy Spirit, we shouldn't expect comfort until its work has been accomplished. Hence, the Scriptures are to be used to enlighten the weary believer that he might cooperate with the Holy Spirit during the process. The Scriptures used may not serve to alleviate present suffering; but when properly understood, suffering will take on its proper perspective and issue in resurrection life, which must necessarily come out of death.

The Scriptures have thus been utilized to get at the core problem—self or flesh—rather than to deal with some of the symptoms, which could possibly prolong the agony.

The counselor's role is to "home in" on those areas of deficiency such as assurance, security, acceptance with which the client may be struggling. Once the impediment is identified, rifle-type Scriptures may be assigned which are appropriate to the need. In addition to remedial Scriptures, those which plot the course ahead are assigned as the Spirit pinpoints the stage of growth attained in the client's life. Such an assessment is prayerfully reached through the interaction of counselor and client under the guidance of the Holy Spirit. In this, as in all other aspects of the counseling process, the counselor and client(s) work together, with first one being led of the Spirit and then the other. The counselor is to lead when it is discovered that the client is moving through terrain over which he has never passed. Study of a particular theme in the Word will continue until the Holy Spirit has taught the needed lesson, and then assignments will be shifted to build upon that which has been solidified.

Occasionally the counselor is faced with a person who can retain nothing that he reads, resulting in his refusal to read and waste his time. Jim was a prime example of this. After several interviews there was little discernible progress and the counselor suggested that counseling be terminated for a period of time. Upon resumption of counseling, the client was informed that he must do the assigned study or further counseling was pointless. He reluctantly agreed to be faithful in the assigned study. The first night he read the assignment and retained absolutely nothing. (His main symptom was obsessive thoughts.) But on the job the next day, the Spirit was faithful to call to his remembrance something he had read the night before. The second night was a repeat performance, as was the next day with some other recollection. The third night he dutifully read his assignment, and the next day the Holy Spirit broke through and released him from the obsessive thoughts. Incidentally, two psychiatrists told him and his wife that he would never be any better and they would "just have to learn to live with it."

"For the word of God is quick, and powerful, and sharper than any twoedged sword, piercing even to the dividing asunder of soul and spirit, and of the joints and marrow, and is a discerner of the thoughts and intents of the heart" (Hebrews 4:12).

The longest chapter in the Bible, Psalm 119, is devoted to the Word, which is God's way of underscoring its importance. Directing a person to the truths he needs to understand from the Word is an exciting venture for counselor and client alike as God in His faithfulness ministers life through the written Word and the Living Word, the Lord Jesus Christ.

Some have faithfully searched the Scriptures for an answer to their dilemma but in vain. As they read the assigned passages during the term of counseling, they tend to interpret them just as in times past, which results in being further disillusioned. Such persons frequently receive a fresh view of the Word by seeing it through the eyes of another person—a counselor or author who describes scriptural truths in a manner with which he can identify. Such is the rationale for the use of literature for spiritual growth, the theme of the next chapter.

9

Literature and Spirituotherapy

The Use of Literature

A word of warning is in order at the very outset of the consideration of the topic. Throughout this book there has been an emphasis on the use of the Word of God in counseling, and the Word is never to be minimized or supplanted by literature, however scripturally sound and enlightening. God speaks only and always through His inspired and infallible Word to the needs of men and to men in need.

Someone has said the Bible sheds a lot of light on commentaries; there are those who decry the use of commentaries or any material other than the Scripture itself. When the Word is truly interpreted to the seeking person by the Holy Spirit as He guides him into all truth (John 16:13), there is no need for illumination provided by man. However, it cannot be denied that God does use human instrumentality or there would be no need for ministers or missionaries; all that would be necessary would be to provide individuals with the Word in their own language and leave the rest to the Spirit of God. This is not to disparage the efficacy of the Word, since the Word itself says that men were called and sent out to spread the Good News as men and women are yet called today.

Literature is to be used in the same manner as the counselor—to aid individuals in understanding how God can meet their needs through the Lord Jesus Christ. Both the literature and the counselor must be steeped in the Word and offer only increased understanding by application of the Word. The author is heavily vested in the use of diagrams as a method of illustrating spiritual truth. The Line diagram in chapter 5 has been used by the Holy Spirit probably more than any other diagram developed by GFI to unlock the truth of identification with Christ to burdened believers.

The instance comes to mind of a missionary couple who came for counseling because of the husband's physical breakdown on the field. After they had been back in the States awhile it was suggested by a friend that they visit GFI for some counseling. The husband was the prime consideration, since the wife seemed to be coping fairly well, at least on the surface. The wife revealed that she had never wanted to go to the mission field because of nagging feelings of inferiority but had dutifully "slugged it out" for three or four terms. She was, by her husband's report, head and shoulders above many of the missionary wives in most areas. She had wanted to be a *minister's* wife but not a *missionary's!*

The counselor used the first half hour as usual, getting acquainted with them and their situation, and then presented the Wheel and Line diagrams for their consideration. As the counselor traced the eternal-life line back to the cross, she broke into tears and sobbed for several minutes as she "saw" her death with Christ and that she was already seated in heavenly places (Ephesians 2:6). Upon returning the next day her inferiority feelings had vanished, and she couldn't wait to return to the mission field in the power of the Spirit!

She had, of course, known and probably had committed to memory most of the Scripture passages used by the counselor that hour; and yet she had never "seen" them under illumination of the Spirit as she did that day. God spoke to her through His Word, but He used a counselor with a few lines on a piece of paper to unlock the meaning of the Word to this sister in Christ.

The author had a similar experience as God used a book, *Victorious Christian Living—Studies in Joshua* by Alan Redpath. It was still the Word of God which was honored as Galatians 2:20 was couched in the pages of this book, and the Spirit of God illuminated this precious and freeing truth. Galatians 2:20 had been committed to memory several years before, but God had not chosen to illuminate it prior to the author's reading it in this setting.

The author has received numerous letters from persons in this country where release from a variety of symptoms has come through an understanding of the truths from Scripture when illustrated diagrammatically. Many have told of dismissing psychiatrists and psychologists with no counseling at all as they understood what the true problem was, self or flesh, and how God had provided the complete answer in the Lord Jesus Christ.

Another case which grips the heart is that of a sweet brother in the Lord, a minister in his late sixties, who was retired because of coronary problems. His ministry had been blessed of the Lord despite severe internal conflict which had been his constant companion for a lifetime. It stemmed back to his parents' divorce in childhood, because of which he was forced to be on his own from his early teens. Rejection had rendered him unable to show love to his first child until several years after her birth. His salvation at about age twenty had helped to some degree, but the emotional scars were to be carried throughout his ministry, with negative effects on his ability to relate to his children, wife, and others.

He fought his way through extensive education, beyond that of the average minister, and was used in the lives of many individuals. He could study the Word in the original languages and had for nearly half a century; but he had never known, experientially, his identification with Christ until his ministry was all but finished on this Earth. God used a lecture explaining rejection and some simple diagrams to release this brother in the Lord, hopefully to begin the ministry anew and to ". . . restore . . . the years that the locust hath eaten . . ." (Joel 2:25).

On and on could go the accounts of God using literature of various kinds and diagrams to open up the Scriptures to hungry hearts. And, then, a double blessing comes when these individuals can turn around and use the same materials to explain the scriptural way of victory to another—to learn to witness to other Christians—where formerly they had nothing to say. One lady who was a Bible-school graduate was married to a minister who dropped out after his first position in a church. She came with some psychosomatic ailments which had disappeared by the time of her second interview, since she entered into victory in the first. Again the Wheel and Line was instrumental in her appropriation of Christ as life. By the time she returned for her third interview about two weeks later, she had already led three ladies into an experimental understanding of identification, using the same material. Again there was no Scripture shared with her that she had not known intellectually before; the difference was the Holy Spirit's illumination where she was taught *spiritually* what she already knew *intellectually*.

The foregoing will serve to illustrate that literature is merely used to give additional insight from a different angle to aid the individual in understanding Scripture which he may have known for years. It is strongly suggested that these diagrams or new ones developed by the counselor be used routinely in the early counseling interviews. It is not to be inferred by the reader that the particular diagrams developed by the author or any others are absolutely essential; in fact, the Holy Spirit was pleased to use no diagram or human instrumentality (other than the aforementioned book) in the author's release near midnight in October 1965. When the inquirer searches with all his heart, he will somehow find the answer (Jeremiah 29:13).

There can be no established order of study of literature along with the Word because no two individuals are alike in their needs nor in their preference for authors and approaches to explanation of spiritual truth. The approach to the use of literature at GFI has been to have books of several authors available which support the scriptural teaching being received during the counseling interviews. The counselor should be thoroughly familiar with his authors and with their books to be able to recommend those that deal with the issues with which his client is grappling at the time. Material which is either behind or ahead of the client's stage of growth will not be useful to him. The early interviews should concentrate on spiritual growth until there is a breakthrough, and then Scripture and literature can be used to deal with problem areas such as marriage, finances, discipline and nurture of children, etc. Jumping into these areas before the spiritual foundation is built can be detrimental, if not disastrous, to the whole counseling process.

Not only should the depth of reading material be considered but also the length. The person who is severely depressed and can't concentrate, or the person who is a poor reader, is unlikely to read a lengthy and scholarly book. Small booklets written for the average reader are much more likely for such a person. At the other extreme, the highly intellectual or gifted person needs material which will challenge him intellectually as well as spiritually. Some will need a study guide for an in-depth study of the Word, where the skeptic may need some excellent apologetic material. One may appreciate material written in a devotional manner, while others profit more by a scholarly treatment of Scripture. The astute counselor must be discerning of his client, his needs, the Scriptures, and available literature as he assays to lead the client to the Truth while avoiding pitfalls which the wrong literature may bring.

The client must be apprised that the suggested literature is merely an aid as the Word is studied and its study is not to eclipse that of Scripture. Also, he must be warned that no author's work is to be accepted in its entirety. Nor are all books of one author endorsed because one (or part of one) is recommended. For instance, the author recommends several of Watchman Nee's books—those compiled from his lectures by others. Many have received great blessings from having read one or more of this brother's books. After having been so blessed, individuals begin to study *The Spiritual Man*, believing it to be Nee's most complete work. However, it was the first and only work actually written by Nee; and it was his desire that the work not be translated, saying it was "too perfect." While there is much that is good in the work, there are also some areas which seem to extrapolate beyond the Scriptures. Some of the positions in the work, especially in volume 3, are not in consonance with his views in his mature years. This is only an example of the weeding out which must be done with the works of *all* authors, *including* the writer's!

What is true of the author's books is true of those of almost all the authors recommended, since the theological terminology and the model of man have not been sufficiently concise to afford consistent and definitive semantics. Some of the best books on spiritual growth are woefully inadequate in this particular. This is one area in which the counselor must be wary and inform his clients that existing literature is consistent in its inconsistency as it regards terminology dealing with the makeup of man. Perhaps one day a compendium of literature may be available to aid in rectifying this situation.

Having lauded literature's strengths and criticized its weaknesses, the author will proceed to commend some authors and certain of their works for the counselor's or would-be counselor's perusal and qualified recommendation to those with whom he ministers. The works are listed under the area for which they are best suited. To repeat for emphasis, *not all of a given book is necessarily endorsed by this author, nor is it to be construed that other works by the same author are recommended.* It may also be that a particular author may hold certain doctrinal positions which are contrary to this author's views; this does not, however, preclude use of that portion of the author's work which is in harmony with this counseling approach. Just because we disagree with *some* of what a person says is certainly not justification for dismissing *all* that he says. It is hoped that the reader will not only be discerning to ferret out error but also open to truth from whatever source! Those books dealing with the psychological aspects of man are commended for *psychological understanding only;* those portions offering answers through therapy—whether via a therapist or self-help—are to be discounted.

Assignments

The literature utilized is to work in close correspondence with the Scripture to enhance the profit from the Word. It may be a study guide of the Word itself or a book or booklet dealing with the same theme. Since the Wheel and Line diagrams of chapter 5 are almost invariably introduced in the first interview, it is extremely profitable for the client to review this material which has been explained to him and study the relevant Scriptures.

Some find it of great value to have a cassette tape of the entire first (or subsequent) interview to listen again to the salient points of the conversation (even his own). The nonreader or the poor reader (as well as a very busy individual) may profit greatly by cassette tapes by selected speakers along the lines of the counseling. A very reliable source of such tapes is Bible Believer's Cassettes, 130 North Spring, Springdale, Arkansas 95014.

The New Life by Captain Reginald Wallis has been found especially helpful after an initial understanding of the Wheel and Line. The first four chapters are particularly fraught with meaning for the earnest seeker. *Rivers of Living Water* by Ruth Paxson, *Principles of Spiritual Growth* by Miles Stanford, and *Victory in Christ* by Charles Trumbull are particularly helpful in the initial stages of counseling. A small booklet, *But How,* by David Tryon is germane also. As counseling continues, *Normal Christian Life* by Watchman Nee is good. As a continuation, *Growth in Grace* by Dr. Victor Matthews is also very helpful!

A small booklet that is good to study along with the Word is *New Testament Living* by Norman B. Harrison. It is convenient to carry in pocket or purse and serves well for group discussion, since questions for discussion of each chapter are provided.

It is better to know a few authors well and to use their books discerningly than to assign a smorgasbord and hope that something will fit somewhere! A selection of works that can be very helpful is arranged by subject in the reading list at the back of this book.

10

Last Things

No, we are not suddenly shifting to eschatology; this is merely where we begin to sign off. Many things have been discussed with none having been treated exhaustively, though the reader may be exhausted.

The work necessary to be done by the Holy Spirit in the life of the counselor and the manner in which he may be used of God to share the Christ-life with another has been described in gross terms. It has not been the purpose of the book to supply detail, since each chapter could easily be expanded into a book in itself. Rather, it is the framework within which the Holy Spirit can supply the details as the trusting believer walks and works in Him. Until the believer has been enlightened as herein described by the working of the Holy Spirit through being driven to the Word by circumstances and inner prompting, volumes could be read without being edifying to the reader. Contrariwise, the Christian who has been so taught by the Spirit of God will find the foregoing material helpful without the benefit of formal counseling training.

Follow-up

An area which is of great concern to the counselor is building upon the foundation laid during the brief time of counseling with an individual. Again, this should (and probably will) be the subject of a book for those pastors and dedicated Christians who would disciple other believers. The person who has been called of God into a ministry of counseling outside of the context of the Church is limited in his resources for follow-up. In fact, this should not be his responsibility but that of the local church.

It is the position of the author and Grace Fellowship International that the bulk of the counseling herein described should be done by the pastor and people in the context of the local church. There are always some situations which a person would find very awkward to reveal to his pastor or brothers and sisters in the church and with which he would be more comfortable with an outsider. The majority of these could be handled by a pastor or counselor in another church, so some swapping can be done to the edification of all concerned.

The Church is the institution which God ordained to meet the needs of saved and unsaved alike. However, until churches begin to let their people know that pastor and people are spiritually equipped to deal with some of the more serious problems with which many are struggling, those within the Church are being forced outside the Church for answers. Too frequently, they are finding substitutes for God's answer in a variety of man's concoctions and are drawn into humanistic (if not hedonistic) diversions which may be a detour at best or a dead end from which they never return.

But what of those who receive Christ-centered counseling as herein described and find victory over sin, marital difficulties, and/or mental/emotional disturbances? Chapter 7 delineates some of the "downers" which may be expected and the absolute necessity of a daily walk in the Spirit if victory is to be maintained. Seven years of experience have proved beyond doubt that short-term counseling, in itself, will not insure long-term victory. To be sure, there is that minority of persons who will study, seek out fellowship, and reckon continuously on their resources in Christ and avoid serious recurrences of former patterns of thinking and behavior. *These are the exception rather than the rule!*

Many of those who have entered into great victory have later had serious regressions and some are again walking "after the flesh." It is with such persons that the counselor's heart is saddened and he begins to ask himself such questions as: Where did I fail this person? Should there have been further counseling? Was there a key spiritual truth which the individual failed to fully appreciate or appropriate? These and a myriad of other questions flood in upon the counselor who loves those with whom he works and has an earnest desire that they continue "walking in truth" (2 John 4).

Upon seeing a person known to have had a life change for a period of time who then reverted to former behavior (or worse), the conventional therapist would have every reason to question the validity of the counseling approach as being fraught with some of the same chronicity which necessarily haunts him. Although there has not been time or funds for systematically checking on the status of those who have received counseling after a period of months or years, the author has known over the years of several with whom he has personally counseled who have later experienced severe problems. Some have returned for counseling and have resolved the problem which caused regression; others continue to walk after the flesh and are living in defeat as their daily portion today.

Does this reflect on God's ability to transform lives and keep them? Not one iota! The failure is on _man's_ part; at times it is the failure of the counselor to instruct the client in the Word to the point where he can maintain victory. In the main, it is the near absence of systematic follow-up which simply cannot be done in a counseling ministry. Neither the time nor the funds are available, and, beyond that, it is not the responsibility of a counseling ministry. What we are talking about is discipling the believer, which is the function of the Church. It is the responsibility of the counselor to direct the client to other believers who can be of help in discipling him. It is precisely here that the counselor finds much difficulty. Rare indeed is the client who can be directed back to his pastor and church with the utmost confidence that the proper nurture from the Word and fellowship with other believers will result in continued victory. With all too many who have a downer after the mountaintop and fall into defeat and/or sin, those in the church are the first to put him down rather than to "put him up" into heavenly places (Ephesians 2:6) where he belongs, since that is where God placed him.

One lady who had entered into great victory informed the counselor that she was going to share with her pastor the blessings God had showered upon her. Since the counselor knew something of the stance of this particular church, she was warned that it might not be received with great elation, to say the least. When she told the pastor what God had done, he replied in a rather gruff voice, "You have to watch these counselors; they will try to get you to leave your church, etc., etc." Rejoicing with her that God had released her from long-standing emotional problems and marital discord was strangely absent. Is it difficult to see that the necessary nurture and follow-up to insure her continued victory would be a problem in such a church? And yet the counselor can ill afford to recommend that such a person change churches, because this pastor was faithful to preach the Word and see people saved. Many churches are very strong in the area of evangelism and very weak in discipleship. It is at this point that such churches must not be condemned (put down) but helped ("put up") that they might be equipped both to disciple Christians and to follow up those who have received counseling elsewhere.

When such follow-up is not available in the client's church, it is advisable to place him (or them) with another individual or couple who can fellowship and study with him (them) without tampering with his (their) church membership. Once such clients are consistent in their walk, they can be a great help to others in their own church. The Word doesn't say *step* in the Spirit; it says, "Walk in the Spirit" (Galatians 5:16). A person may take the step of appropriating Christ as life and then not follow through. A child may take his first step, but he still has not learned to walk; he will probably fall flat on his face many times before he walks consistently. The same is true of the believer who takes the step of appropriating his identification with Christ; he will undoubtedly fall flat on his face several times before walking consistently in victory. When he does, it is vital that he have a more mature believer who can help him get up and walk again. Even *Christians* who do not understand will inadvertently kick him in the face while he is down, because they have no idea how to pick him up. When they have not dealt with the flesh in their own lives they are not sympathetic to his particular "brand" of flesh, and are spiritually unprepared to be of help. Since they have not scaled the heights from which he fell, they can not help him retrace his steps or realize the full impact of his fall.

Despite its failures and shortcomings, the author has by no means given up on the Church and its God-given mandate to "teach all nations . . . to observe *all* things . . ." (Matthew 28:19, 20, *italics added*) that He has commanded us. Rather, there must be the edifying of the Church through the renewal of the Holy Spirit that it might be a haven for the defeated, disturbed Christian as well as the place where the person who is lost might find the way to the Savior.

A Friendly Warning

Those who enter into victory after years of defeat in the Christian life are acutely aware that most of their brothers and sisters in Christ desperately need the answer they have found. Many have a new zeal analogous to that of a new Christian and set out to "stamp out the ignorance" in their acquaintances. Those who are about to go down for the third time may be very receptive, but the majority will almost visibly have out the No Help Wanted sign. The rebuffs a person gets in his initial attempts to witness to Christians are very much like those he received from unbelievers upon attempting to win them to Christ.

The writer recalls a lady with whom he counseled and who entered into victory after the first interview. She had been on tranquilizers for almost two decades. Her husband had not been able to come with her, as she was from a town some distance away. She was asked what she was going to tell her husband; her reply was, "If he can't see it, it isn't worth talking about!" He did "see it" and came with her for an interview as she returned a month or two later. (She had a total of three interviews in the first series before returning home.) Between her first and second trips to Denver her brother from another state was in her home for about forty-eight hours. She told him nothing about the counseling but he saw such a transformation from the way he had remembered her that he asked, "What has happened to you that you're so different?" This same lady began helping others almost immediately.

Teaching truths in a class or from the pulpit will frequently draw fire from those who do not understand; the cross cuts across the flesh and the flesh reacts—occasionally with hostility. The Holy Spirit must give great discernment as to when these truths may be introduced and the emphasis which may be attached to such teaching. Churches have been known to split because the pastor clearly taught the Cross and the people were unprepared for the "meat of the Word." Spiritual indigestion may be the cause of many rumbles in the Church.

Individually or in the Church, it is necessary for the person(s) newly understanding union or identification with Christ to *live* Christ. Others cannot be forced to drink but they can become thirsty for what they see in an abiding, victorious believer. We can witness to the abundant life that God has given and the transformation He has wrought in our lives without "laying it on" those with whom we have opportunity to share.

The pastor also will do well to exercise great caution as he begins to teach these truths. As a rule, there are only a small percentage of those in a given church who have been prepared by the Holy Spirit and circumstances to receive "the Word with all readiness of mind" (Acts 17:11). An experiential understanding of these truths will permeate all messages, but making the growth truths the central focus of all messages would result in not teaching the whole counsel of God.

Discipleship or growth groups can be an excellent place to emphasize spiritual growth without alienating those who may not realize their need. Also, a Sunday-school class for new members can include the basic teaching on identification with Christ to good advantage. There are those in every church with the necessary spiritual gifts to provide help to those who are defeated and in despair, if only the opportunities were available for those who have these gifts to identify and learn to exercise them. God has made the gifts available in every group of believers, and it is only the Spirit-controlled believer who will know his spiritual gift and be able to utilize it in the Body of Christ.

Conclusion

Though much has been said, even more has been unsaid. It is the author's prayer that the insights given by the Holy Spirit through His inerrant Word may be utilized in the lives of multiplied thousands who, in turn, may be used to set God's people free and to win the lost to Him.

> Now unto him that is able to keep you from falling, and to present you faultless before the presence of his glory with exceeding joy.
>
> Jude 24

Amen.

Appendix

Transcript of an Actual
Counseling Interview

Appendix

Transcript of an actual interview with names and places changed and used by permission of the client with the concurrence of her parents. Some other details also have been changed to insure anonymity.

C (*the counselor*)

J (*the client,* Judy)

C: Hello, I'm Dr. _____.

J: I'm Judy Brown.

C: It's good to meet you, Judy. [*Walking into office*] Why don't you have a seat so we can get acquainted? If you will, sit in the chair nearest the desk, since I like to use diagrams as we talk.

J: Okay.

C: Now, how old are you, Judy?

J: Eighteen.

C: Just finish high school?

J: Uh-huh.

C: What high school?

J: Central Christian School.

C: And what church do you attend?

J: Central Christian.

C: How did you hear about us?

J: Through a friend; her name is Pat Smith.

C: How long have you known Pat?

J: I worked for her a couple of days through an agency that I work for; she told me about your place here.

C: Oh, great. And what's going on right now—why did you decide to come in?

J: I was having some trouble deciding where to go to college in the fall, and she said, "It'd be a good idea if you'd just go in and talk to him and see what he has to say." And so I thought I might as well—I have nothing to lose.

C: So no big thing is going on as far as emotional problems or things of that nature? You're primarily concerned with choosing a college and career?

J: Right. There is some pressure involved from different areas to promote different schools, and that's about it.

C: What schools are you considering?

J: It's between Christian U and City Baptist.

C: And the pressure is partly because your pastor is on the board of one of the colleges?

J: Right.

C: What do you know about Christian?

J: Very little. I visited the college twice; and at first I wasn't impressed with it at all. It isn't on a campus and it lacks the things that a college has or—you usually look for in a college. It's located in downtown Centerville and I wasn't impressed with what I saw. And then I got to dating Jim, who's going there, and he'll be going there in the fall; and he said, "You ought to look into it"; he says, "I don't see real peace in your heart about City." And so I thought, well, maybe he's right—because I knew the peace wasn't there that I needed for City. I began to pray about it and really ask the Lord and it seemed like such a turmoil; I didn't feel a peace about either one. I thought it wouldn't work for me to stay home, then; and I just didn't feel a peace about either college.

C: Have you thought about looking at some other alternative colleges or . . . ?

J: Uh-uh, those were the only two that really interested me in business.

C: Business is what you definitely want for a major?

J: Yes.

C: Any idea of full-time service—or do you just want to get a Christian education?

J: Full-time service, probably.

C: What would you do in full-time service of a business nature? What are you considering?

J: A preacher's wife is what I'm looking into.

C: Then you've got to find the preacher, too!

J: Right! [*Both laugh*]

C: So, then, you'll get to be the pastor's wife and you'll run the business, huh? But he's not really on the horizon—not yet?

J: Well, Jim is attending Christian, too.

C: How long have you been going with him?

J: Since about May.

C: Is he from Central too?

J: Yes, he is.

C: Okay. [*Changing the subject*] What kind of family do you have—brothers and sisters?

J: I have two sisters, one's twelve and one's five, and my parents have been active in the church since I was little. My dad has been a deacon and my parents are both Sunday-school teachers.

C: There's six years, then, between you and the next one.

J: Right.

C: So you are something like an only child. Could you relate to your parents?

J: Sort of.

C: You can't have too much fellowship with your sisters because of the age difference, huh?

J: Right.

C: Which parent would you say you're closer to?

J: My mom.

C: Can you talk to her about most anything?

J: Uh-huh.

C: Do you?

J: Yes, as much as I can.

C: Is there freedom in the conversation?

J: Yes.

C: What kind of relationship with your dad?

J: Oh, it's a very shaky one. There was an accident that happened when I was a child and my arm was broken; and since this time it put such an impression in his life that "she [Judy] is off at a distance. She's something that I just can't relate to." He was never taught to love in the home. It's been hard for him to communicate with me and I really had to work at it. He's just moody. I know when I've been on a trip or something and I'd call him long distance and say, "Dad, I love you," and he'd go, "Yeah." He didn't mean to sound brusque; but it was just the way that he said it that it hurt. It cut and I felt—well, should I keep trying until it quits hurting? And that's what I've had to do—just to keep trying because he's so cold inside; I have very little relationship with him at all. We don't say any more than a paragraph of words to each other in a month's time; we just don't speak to each other. So it's very distant.

C: How do you feel toward other men? Is it difficult for you to relate to boys once they start getting close? Is that a problem?

J: No, it doesn't bother me. I don't really have that many girl friends; it's mostly the guys that I run around with—the guys are the ones that I sit with in church and go out for pizza with and stuff afterwards. It isn't really the girls.

C: So it hasn't really hurt you, then, as far as relating to men?

J: [*Nods*]

C: So you've never quite felt that your dad accepted you?

J: Right.

C: He doesn't know how to?

J: I don't think so.

C: How did he grow up? Do you know?

J: I know his parents argued a lot—and since he's saved, and the rest of his brothers aren't, he's been put aside as an outcast in the family.

C: At what age? Do you know?

J: Well, this was when he was out of the home, but other than that I don't know much about it. I just know that his mother and father didn't show love in the home toward him; and therefore he couldn't show it toward his brothers and sisters. It's been hard for him to show love, but it's gradually been coming.

C: Were his brothers and sisters the same way—as far as relating to the parents? Or do you think he felt like the black sheep?

J: I think he felt like the black sheep.

C: Was he oldest, youngest—or where was he in the lineup?

J: He's the secondborn.

C: He never did quite make it with either one of his parents?

J: Right.

C: What about relating to your mother . . . can he show her love? Do you ever see him show affection to her?

J: Not really—not a whole lot—not an overabundance like I see in other families, you know; it isn't real evident.

C: There are no boys in your family—two sisters; can he relate to either one of your sisters?

J: Oh, we've had trouble with that, too. The secondborn—she feels the same way—that he just can't accept her. And now that the little one has come, she feels that he favors her; and he is very proud of her. It's just that . . . it's always that we're striving to please Dad, striving to please him and we never can. It's been this way through high school with my grades—always trying to get the straight A's—trying to get the best grades I can; and it never seemed to please him. And it just . . . you know, you think, "Well, why try? I'm just gonna have to give up." And yet you know you can't because you've got to continue to try and please him.

C: You never can make it, so you perhaps feel like there's a bar that you try to measure up to—and as soon as you get up there, he raises the bar. Then you feel—it's an impossible situation! Do you love him?

J: Yes, very much.

C: Love him enough to try to get some love back?

J: Right.

C: Do you think he loves you?

J: I think he does.

C: But just can't show it?

J: He just can't show it. It's just bottled up inside. He's expressed it a few times and it sets me back because I'm just not used to having it. And it's just little things—such as special times of the year, like graduation this year. He was just excited that the relatives had come out and things, and he came up and hugged me; and he said, "I'm proud of you." And it just brought tears to my eyes because I didn't know how to react to it; it was the first time in so long he had showed me love that way.

C: Well, do you think he recognizes this as a problem?

J: Not really. I just think he has accepted it as his way of life.

C: He doesn't think it can be any different?

J: No, I don't think so. That's just the way he was brought up.

C: Does he know you're here?

J: I think so.

C: If you suggested that he come and look at his relationship with you or to see how to express love, how do you think he'd react?

J: I think his pride would be hurt.

C: Do you think he'd do it?

J: I don't know; it might take some convincing.

C: How does he relate to the pastor?

J: Very well.

C: If his pastor suggested he come, what do you think he'd say?

J: I think he'd say he would, but inside he'd be fighting a battle.

C: I'm sure your pastor would advise him to come. He has been wanting to come for a workshop and hasn't been able to make it yet. Most people, like your dad, don't know that they can get rid of hangups and learn to express love. He just thinks, "That's the way I am, and I have to fight it and do the best I can." What about reading? Would he read something that you suggest?

J: He doesn't do a lot of reading. He just . . . he's more the outdoors type—in the yard and things. He might, but to get him to read would really be a struggle. It just isn't in his line of thinking.

C: What kind of work does he do?

J: He's an electrician.

C: So far as the family is concerned, this is the biggest thing you've got going—not being able to relate to him?

J: Right.

C: [*Changing the subject*] Now how do you feel about yourself? Do you like yourself?

J: I've accepted myself, I guess, for what I am.

C: For what you are or for what you are to the Lord?

J: What I am; what I am to the Lord I haven't accepted.

C: Do you ever feel inferior?

J: Very much.

C: Do you ever wonder why?

J: Uh-huh.

C: Do you know why at all?

J: That . . . ?

C: That you feel inferior.

J: No, not really.

C: Has your dad made you feel like the greatest all the time you were growing up?

J: [*Shakes head*]

C: Can you see how that would affect you, whether he says it in words or not? All of your life he has communicated to you in subtle ways: "You're a loser; you can't make it!'' If he hasn't given you a sense of worth, he has made you feel *worthless.*

J: Right, but I've always been striving to prove him wrong.

C: *Are* you inferior?

J: I don't think so.

C: But you *feel* inferior.

J: I *feel* it; but I know that I'm not.

C: So with your mind you *know;* but with your feelings, it's a different story. Some things that you attempt to do, you probably feel as though you can't. You know you can and you go ahead and do it; but you still *feel* as though you can't.

J: Right.

C: Do you ever feel as though you can't do something after you've already got it finished?

J: [*Nods yes*]

C: Sort of silly, isn't it? But this background of not learning a sense of worth is where the inferiority thing comes from. How about with your mom? Does she ever really affirm to you that you are okay, that you can do things well at home?

J: She just knows that I have the capabilities. She always says, ''You've got the potential to do it, and you'll do it.'' And there, too, it's always been, Get the grades so Mom and Dad'll praise you. You know, Get their OK; get their acceptance—but it never came. My sister is the one that doesn't make the grades.

C: She doesn't have any way of making it at all, does she?

J: She's the secondborn of the family. She has no desire; she wants to be a social being. She doesn't care about schoolwork; she doesn't . . . all she's concerned about is the boys! And she's in school and all she does is *goof* and the teachers see it. So she comes home with the bad grades; and she gets a D, brings it up to a C, and she gets the praise; and I stay at straight A's and nothing is said because it's expected of me.

C: You can't show an improvement, huh? Apparently, you

haven't rebelled a lot. What about the twelve-year-old? Is she beginning to rebel?

J: She began a long time ago. She's very rebellious.

C: It's just a matter of time until she really gets into some trouble?

J: That's right.

C: And then your dad might say, "How can she do this to me? I've done *everything* for her. She "acts out" and you "act in" some—keep it all in. Ever get a little depressed?

J: Yes. Sometimes I just get in the car, drive away, and pretend like it isn't there. That seems to be the best way to escape it all. To me, Cathy, the secondborn, seems to be leeching off Mom and Dad. It's whatever she can get out of 'em. I've always been a very independent person; you work for what you want. You go out and you make your own money; and, therefore, you'll have the money for this, that, and the other thing; and you've got your money for the things that you want. [*Quoting parents*] "We're not gonna pay for it. If you want, you know . . . put gas in the car if you go out and make the money for it; we're not gonna give it to you." With Cathy it's just the opposite. She's gotta have money for this activity, for that activity. And Mom and Dad haven't really got it and I hate to see her sit there and soak them for everything they're worth, and it just . . . she has no gratitude at all! And if Mom and Dad *do* give me money, you know, I want to thank them for it because I know it comes hard, because I've been out working. But she doesn't care; she just has a no-care attitude; that's the brand across her forehead: NO CARE.

C: Do you think maybe she's saying to her parents by the way she acts: "You have rejected me so I'll reject you"? And she gets what she can?

J: Yes.

C: She can't please them anyway so she's saying, "Hang it on your nose; I'll do my thing."

J: Right.

C: [*Changing subject*] When were you saved?

J: When I was five.

C: If you hadn't had the Lord to depend on, you'd have been in a pretty good mess, wouldn't you?

J: Right.

C: What if I said to you that you're very attractive? What's your reaction?

J: That it isn't true.

C: I sort of expected that. How many guys do you think you could get to agree with that?

J: Probably quite a few.

C: You know better than that!

J: But I still say it isn't true.

C: Because you don't feel beautiful, do you? So your feelings control your attitude *toward yourself* even though, objectively, you *know* you're not inferior because you make straight A's. You would have a pretty hard time getting a lot of guys to say you are unattractive—because you *are* a very attractive gal, and you know that. But you can't admit it because you don't *feel* beautiful. Aside from the rejection by your dad, your relationship with your mom is somewhat of a performance kick, too. To make it with her, you still have to perform.

J: Right.

C: So there's a little bit of it with her. It's pretty hard to sit back and know that you're accepted without *doing*. What about with the Lord? Do you have to perform to get His acceptance?

J: No, not that I know of.

C: But do you behave that way? Are you in a "works" thing trying to make it with the Lord so that you're sure that He loves you?

J: Not really.

C: What if you miss your devotions one day, or miss church?

J: I feel horrible!

C: Why?

J: Because I know it's expected of me, I guess.

C: Who expects it?

J: The Lord.

C: He must be frowning! See what I mean?

J: Right. You have me cornered!

C: Carries over a little, huh?

J: Right.

C: Besides the rejection by your dad and a little bit by your mom, what has been going on in your life up to now? What happened between the ages of six and twelve? Any bad things that happened to you that caused a lot of guilt or fear or anything that really bugs you?

J: Not that I can think of.

C: During those years, did you have a lot of friends at school?

J: Yes. It is a small school, so it was easy to make friends.

C: How long have you been at Christian?

J: Five years.

C: Where were you earlier than that, during elementary school? In public school?

J: Yes, public school.

C: Did you feel in those earlier years like you were part of the group, or part of the gang?

J: Not really. Because I was always the one that had to wear the dresses down and I was the one that couldn't participate in the dances and things; and I was, therefore, set aside. I was marked, you know, as someone being different even when I was little.

C: So your peer relationships have resulted in rejection?

J: Right. The teachers accepted me because of my grades. I was always bragged on by the teachers—but, you know, the kids wouldn't have a whole lot to do with me, which never really bothered me because that was the way I wanted it—then.

C: That (rejection) was all you knew?

J: Right.

C: They loved and accepted you the way your dad did (on a performance basis). You wouldn't know what to do with love if you had it! Performance is the big deal to you; you're accepted *if.*

J: Uh-huh.

C: What happens when your performance is accepted and you get straight A's? Do you feel good about that?

J: Not really. It doesn't do anything for me. And I feel like, "Oh, I've made my mark," you know. Big deal!

C: But you still feel the same way inside?

J: Uh-huh.

C: If I can do it, anyone can!

J: That's right.

C: The inferiority feelings still bug you. Now, what about after age twelve—say twelve to eighteen—junior high and high school? Did you have more friends, fewer friends, feel less inferior or more inferior?

J: I'd say I had more friends, because I was in a Christian society.

C: Christian school?

J: Right. It was easier to make friends because you weren't set apart—as strange or even different— because you wore the same type of clothing; everybody looked alike.

C: You *all* looked strange!

J: Right. [*Laughter*]

C: Anything in particular about those years that was outstanding?

J: The thing that impresses me, I guess, about my high-school years is that I started to date a guy when I was in my sophomore year. He was twenty; and, to me, it was something fascinating, you know, like someone accepted me for *me.* Mom and Dad didn't approve, but it didn't really matter to me whether they approved or not. I didn't take it into consideration, you know, when I *should have* because I knew I was out of the Lord's will, because I didn't have the approval of my parents.

When I started dating—I dated him for about two years—and Mom and Dad finally asked me to break up with him; and it just got so bad that I couldn't take their pressure anymore and so I said, "Okay, this is it; I'm just going to break it off with him." So I did. And they were pushing toward another guy that I knew and they wanted me to like him. "He's got a good name in the church; and he makes good money, and you ought to like him." And I said, "Mom, if you'd stay out of it!" And Dad was the same way. They'd push, push, push! Break up with this guy, you know, go with this one. So I broke up with him and I feel if Mom and Dad had stayed out of it like they should have, things would have naturally worn off; things, you know, were just—we were getting tired of each other anyway; and things would have gradually worn to a frazzle and broken off. But they interfered, and in order to gain their acceptance again I went with this other guy—his name was Jim—for about a year. He went off to college in the fall and I waited for him and he came back at Christmas and he had another girl. I wasn't prepared for it and I went through five months of bitterness; and I just grew such a hate in my heart for him—and against my parents, too, for what they had done. They had pushed him on me when I didn't really want it. And I just felt like they were meddling in my affairs when it was my doing because I was the one that had to go with him; I broke up with him at Christmas, like I said, and the bitterness—I just lost so much time and so much effectiveness for the Lord because of the bitterness I had in my heart. And he came home from college in June and it just got to the point where I was just miserable in everything. I'd see the kind of car he drove on the highway and I'd just start screaming inside; and I'd get mad every time someone would mention his name in class and just little things that would just flare my temper up something horrible. He came home in June, and I knew I had to

talk to him and get this out of my system. So I asked him
if I could talk to him one night after church and I said,
"Jim, you know as well as I do that I've had a lot of
bitterness in my heart," and I said, "I've come to ask
your forgiveness." I got it all out; and I just feel,
though, that if Mom and Dad had stayed out of it, and
I'm doing the same thing with—I'm dating another guy
now whose name is Jim, also—and they're pushing
again. I don't know why; it seems like they're trying to
get me out of the house early! I know that's not their
intention but it seems like that's what they're trying to
do; and I said, "Mom, what's the big rush? I'm only
eighteen." "I know; I don't want you to get married for
another five years." I said, "Then why are you *pushing*
me?" "Oh, you'll like him . . . he's got a better"—you
know—"standing with people . . . and he's got a good
personality; he's got this and he doesn't have this, and
he doesn't have this . . . ."

C: Trying to play Holy Spirit?

J: Yeah, and they're just pushing and there's so many
complications with the Jim that I'm dating now. He has
so many convictions that I don't have; and he has so
many standards that he wants a girl to have, and I just
don't have them.

C: Just like your dad?

J: Yes, and I just feel that's not me; he doesn't like the
Judy that's really there; he likes somebody else that he
has made up and we discussed it and he says that's not
the way it is.

C: You'll have to perform just like you did for your dad to
get his acceptance.

J: That's right. And in order to get Jim to accept me, he
doesn't want me to wear pants; he doesn't want me to
wear makeup; he doesn't think girls should work when
they get married; he wants *twelve kids;* all these *ridiculous* sets of ideas. All these ridiculous things and I said,
"Wow, this just *can't be!*" And I've always been
brought up just the opposite, you know, that if

there's an occasion, girls wear pants; and it's become a common trend in society for girls to wear makeup—and just things that seem absurd to me.

C: You still going with him?

J: Yes.

C: Why?

J: I don't know.

C: Because you don't know anybody else yet?

J: Well, we were on a college tour in May and he—he's twenty—he drove a bus and we stopped at the college that Jim Jones (that's the other Jim, the first Jim), we stopped at the college where he was. I got a chance to talk to him a little bit there and he noticed that I was having trouble, you know, trying to get over this thing with Jim. So he talked to me and he said, "Until you start praising the Lord, you're not going to be able to forget what's happened and you're just going to let it eat at you." So I thought, Okay, he's right. So I started praising the Lord and eventually got over it after I thought I never would. His help turned out to be more than just help. When we got back to town we started to date each other. He's a stamp collector, and so the third day that I knew him, here he comes with all these gifts: stamps from this country and that—very valuable. It seemed like he was buying my friendship; and I didn't know how to say, Wait a minute; I don't even like you, you know. I just stood there and let him pour it all on because it was, you know, *anybody* enjoys gifts. So in my room I have over a thousand dollars worth of stamps and he's in Mexico; he has been for two months and he's coming home the first of August and I'm just like standing in the background watching it all roll by because I don't know what to do.

C: Sounds like you can get your degree in business and go into the stamp business, huh? [*Laughter*]

J: Right.

[*Transition from history to interpretation of the Taylor-Johnson Temperament Analysis Test*]

C: Well, that pretty much brings us up to where you are at
      present. Let's look at your test and see how you de-
      scribe yourself here. Since all you need to do is make a
      decision about going to school, there's nothing else
      bugging you, right? Isn't that what you said? [*Chuckles*]

J: I think so.

C: Here's what the test looks like. You rated yourself with
      a 3 on the attitude score, which is really a "lie" scale.
      Four to 7 is neutral; and you rated yourself with a 3,
      which shows you tended to put yourself down a little
      bit—the first time you've *ever* done that, right? [*Grins*]

J: No.

C: The dark gray here is excellent. That's where the blue
      line *should* be. You go *through* it a few times, but you
      don't seem to *stop! Nervousness* is up in the "im-
      provement desirable" area. *Depression*—knocking the
      top out! Sort of an uptight gal. These three things up
      here—social, expressive, sympathetic—these are the
      outgoing traits; and you say, outgoing, you're not! You
      tend to be a loner. If you let people get too close to you,
      all they do is hurt you. So you stay away from them.

J: That's *exactly* right!

C: And then the "expressive–responsive" category—you
      can't express your feelings; you keep everything inside.
      The more you say to people, the more they've got to use
      against you.

J: That's right.

C: You just keep it all in and you're sort of indifferent to
      other people—"I've got enough problems of my own;
      don't bug me with yours."

J: Right.

C: You seem to be pretty much controlled by your feelings,
      since the test shows you to be highly subjective: "I *feel*
      inferior; therefore, I'm going to *act* inferior." The *feel-
      ing* controls you. Other people say, "Why don't you
      do this or that?" Get up and make a ten-minute talk.
      Would you like to do that? [*Judy shakes no*] Why?

Because of the way you feel. You have a fairly strong personality (dominant)—in the acceptable range. Hostility shows "improvement urgent" but you are fairly self-disciplined. What are you going to do with that much hostility? You can't sock someone or they won't especially like you. And you can't say it because you don't have the words; so you keep it inside and drive down the road and scream inside and get depressed and cry. You tend to be sort of upside down inside; you don't like *you* because you feel like your dad doesn't like you.

[*Transition to presenting the answer*]

Now, let's see what God wants to do in your life before He can show you which school you are to attend. People at Christian and City—they have enough trouble without you, already! [*Smiles*] What He wants to do is flip you right side up and get this all straightened out, and then He can show you where He wants you to go to college. If you go there like this and continue to work to try to prove something to somebody, you won't enjoy it anyway. You'll be too busy trying to prove something. When you can rest inside and quit trying to perform, and let Christ do the performing, then this mess gets changed and you will have peace inside. Now, let's look at the scriptural principles that God uses to get this changed around so that you'll be rid of the anxiety. What does Philippians 4:6, 7 say? Have you memorized that?

J: I can't quote it right off.

C: Be *careful* or be *anxious* for nothing; don't *have* anxiety. But you have some! Why? Because you don't know
       how God makes His peace a reality within you. As a Christian you've never found out how Christ could meet your needs.

J: I've always felt independent; I can do it *myself!* Someone put the idea in my head that God gives you a brain to think for yourself; and therefore you should use it. Stand on your own and do your own thing and the Lord will move you one way or another if He wants you to do anything different. That isn't necessarily how it should be.

C: You've been trying to do it yourself and it hasn't worked the best in the world, has it? Okay, let's see how it could be otherwise. Have you ever read this book, *The Handbook of Happiness?*

J: I have it at home; but I haven't read it.

C: Did Pat give it to you?

J: No, another friend that visited you gave it to me.

C: Might be a good idea if you'd read it, huh? You might get your dad to read it. The Word says in 1 Thessalonians 5:23 that we're made up of spirit, soul, and body. What's your soul? [*Pointing to the Wheel diagram*]

J: Oh, I couldn't give an actual answer; I don't know.

C: You know what your body is?

J: Uh-huh.

C: Well, a dog and a cat have a soul, right?

J: I don't know. I don't think so.

C: The soul consists of the mind, emotions, and will, otherwise known as the personality.

J: Oh!

C: Can a dog learn?

J: Yes.

C: Do you ever see a dog get his feelings hurt?

J: Yes.

C: Can he obey or disobey?

J: Yes.

C: He has a soul just like you do. He has a personality or psychological makeup, but he doesn't have a spirit. Now, when your soul was saved, where did the "saving" take place—in what part of you?

J: Spirit?

C: Yes, spirit. So your soul is saved in your spirit. But before you were born again you couldn't relate to God, could you? Your spirit was dead to God [Ephesians 2:1] right? You had a functioning spirit that could relate to Satan, but you couldn't relate to God because you had no relationship with God. There is an interaction that takes place between the body and the soul. Physically, if you get down—have the flu or something like that—it can get you down emotionally, too. And, psychologically, if you've gone through rejection like you have with your dad, and somewhat with your mom, then you can reject yourself and feel bad about yourself; and, eventually, you might get enough conflict in the personality to cause a headache. Have you ever had a problem like that?

J: Uh-huh.

C: Or possibly a nervous stomach?

J: Uh-huh.

C: So you know what that is?

J: Uh-huh.

C: There is also an interaction between the spirit and the soul. If you don't know how God can meet the needs in the soul through your spirit, you really have a spiritual problem.

J: Uh-huh.

C: Your dad, feeling inferior and insecure, doesn't know that he has a need to see how God can work in his life and that all of this can go away. Most Christians don't. Now that's what I want to show you—how to get rid of these inferiority feelings so that they don't affect your life and the way you relate to your dad. The first thing we're interested in is if you're born again. [*Pointing to the "Spirit" portion of the Wheel*] You say you were born again at the age of five.

J: Uh-huh.

C: What about assurance of salvation? Has that ever been a problem?

J: When I was young, but I was told just to rely on the date—I mean on the time. I knew that I was saved and just to trust the Lord that that's what exactly happened. And so I just accepted it from then on.

C: But now your feelings are messed up, so sometimes you could *feel* unsaved even though you *know* you *are* saved?

J: Uh-huh.

C: But you can go back to that time, based on God's Word, and know you're saved.

J: Uh-huh.

C: Fine. What about security—knowing you're going to stay saved?

J: That's mainly not been a problem, because of God's Word.

C: But what about acceptance with God? Do you know that He'll accept you even though you miss devotions or you don't get to church sometimes or—that He accepts you completely whether you perform or not?

J: [*Shakes no*]

C: It's a problem, huh?

J: Uh-huh.

C: What about total surrender, total commitment? Have you ever come to the place that you—where you have totally sold out hook, line, and sinker—given your body as a living sacrifice?

J: I have gone through the motions but I know inside it was because of emotions and not because that's exactly what I wanted to do.

C: Let's describe what I mean and see that we're communicating. A lot of people get the idea that if you totally surrender to God then you have to go into full-time service.

J: That's the impression I've always gotten.

C: The next stop is Bible college. Some people think you surrender to preach—that's full surrender—or to be a missionary. But this commitment or surrender that we're talking about is abandoning all rights to ourselves. I'm willing to stay single the rest of my life, Lord—*Tilt!* Or, I'm willing to marry; or, I'm willing to have *twelve kids!*

J: That's going a little far!

C: Whatever the Lord wants. You sign a blank check, turn over your life and the Lord fills in the amount. It won't cost you *anything;* it'll cost you *everything.* Afterward, you no longer have any rights to make any decisions about yourself. You yield your rights to the Lord and trust Him to be your life and let Him show you what He wants. And whatever He wants, you're satisfied with. It's a decision you make! Now, your emotions may not agree. It's just like when a man and woman get married; they say, "I do," and the preacher says, "You're man and wife." They've made a decision that changes the whole course of their lives. *This* decision is to give your body as a living sacrifice. But, then, the Holy Spirit has to begin to make changes from the inside so that you can do what He wants done. Do you see that it is a decision which you make?

J: Yes.

C: Okay. Now, we can be saved and even make the decision of total surrender and have the Lord Jesus Christ *in* our lives; and He may not be the *center* of the life. If He isn't the center of the life, something else is. The *S* at the center might represent some person. In a negative sort of way your dad is the center of your life, because he largely has caused you to feel the way you do about yourself, hasn't he? Since you don't feel like he has accepted you, you really haven't accepted yourself . . .

J: Right.

C: . . . the way you are, the way you look, the way God made you. When you're not satisfied with the way you look, for instance, you are really saying, "Yes, Lord, I'm the *first* mistake You ever made." In a negative way your parents can be the center of your life. Or, it could be some person like a boyfriend. For a few months there this twenty-year-old, whom you were dating and who dropped you, was the center of your life. Or, the *S* can represent some *thing;* it could also be *success.* It could be performance—trying to get somebody's acceptance. Money, material things—in back of all that, what really is the center of your life?

J: Self.

C: Trying to do it yourself.

J: Uh-huh.

C: Or, another word for that is *flesh.* We are controlling our own lives or letting the flesh control us. And when that is true, the things that have bugged us all of our lives (in the soul portion of the Wheel)—feelings of inferiority—you don't need too much explanation on that, do you?

J: Uh-uh.

C: Feeling insecure; feeling inadequate. Feelings that you've had about yourself, such as guilt. There are two basic types of guilt: There's real guilt, which is caused by sin. What about imaginary guilt—false guilt? You may have thought sometime, "Well, if my dad can't show me love and acceptance, I . . . shouldn't have been born; he'd have been better off without me." You feel guilty for being there and grow up with a case of the "guilties" for even being a person! You might feel like you're breathing somebody else's air, taking up their space or something like that. Now, that's false guilt; and you can go to the altar and confess, but it won't help— because it's not *your* sin that caused the false guilt. Until *self* is dealt with, the false guilt is going to remain. Then, worry, doubts, fear—[*facetiously*] you've never had any of these—you put all that mess together and it becomes frustration. You're frustrated and upset and you come home with A's and your dad doesn't say a thing about it; and you get a little hostile. What are you going to do with it? He's bigger than you are. You

can't haul off and clobber him one! Or your boyfriend drops you.

J: I get it in *every* direction!

C: You get hostile and you'd like to sock it to somebody,
but if you do you won't be accepted. So what you do is
start to beat up yourself, keep it inside, and get depressed.

J: Yes.

C: So depression and anxiety become a way of life. Anxiety shows up here, and depression, so you stay away
from people. Some people can handle it mentally and do
some fantasy; they sit around and daydream.

J: Yes!

C: Now, if you keep that going long enough—stay out in a
dreamworld long enough—it helps, temporarily. Some
become schizophrenic or have obsessive thoughts;
these are mental cop-outs that a person sometimes uses
when he can't face reality. These are mental and emotional cop-outs that we usually keep going because we
don't know what to do with them. As the heat builds up
outside, the pressure builds up *inside.* When that pressure builds up, what are you going to do about it? If you
heat a vessel and don't vent it, it will blow its lid. That's
what happens to a lot of people; they blow their lids.
Others don't get their hostility out, so they take it out on
themselves! Instead of exploding, they implode and
blow a hole in their stomachs; some get a headache or
eat or sleep too much. Sounds like some of those things
happen to you?

J: They do.

C: Some have a spastic colon or rapid heartbeat. In fact, a
lot of things can happen in our body because of the
conflict that's going on in the personality. You can go to
a medical doctor, and he can give you some things to
calm those things down in the body a little bit.

J: But the problem is still there.

C: But the problem is still there! You can go to a
        psychologist or psychiatrist and he works on things in
        the personality, but the problem is *still* there. How do
        you deal with this *self problem* so you can get rid of the
        conflict in the personality? Because that's where the
        problem is. Let's look at the Line diagram. The horizon-
        tal line in the diagram represents eternal life. Eternal life
        is whose life?

J: Our life, if we have accepted Christ.

C: It's our life—but where do we get it?

J: Christ.

C: Okay. So whose life, really, is it?

J: Christ's life.

C: Christ's life. Now, what is eternal life—how long does it
        last?

J: Forever.

C: Does it have any beginning?

J: Uh-uh.

C: Jesus' life has no beginning; He pre-existed; but two
        thousand years ago He took on a human body. The life
        He lived in that body when He entered time is the same
        life He had always been living. And now He lived in a
        different form—the form of man. And how long did He
        live in that body?

J: Thirty-three years.

C: And then what happened to Him?

J: He was crucified.

C: And then what happened?

J: He arose.

C: He rose again and He's still living today—an eternal
        existence. But when you were born you weren't in His
        life at all, were you?

J: Uh-uh.

C: You were in another life here [*pointing to the diagonal
        line, emanating from Adam*]; you were in your parents
        before you were born. And they were in their parents

before they were born. So what would have happened to you if your grandfather had died when he was two years old?

J: I wouldn't be born.

C: You would have shown up missing, huh? He was in his grandfather, and *he* was in *his* grandfather all the way back to that *great* grandfather, Adam. So when Adam was walking around in the Garden of Eden, where were you? Suppose Adam and Eve had died without having any children. Do you think this place would have been a little lonely? We wouldn't have many friends, would we?

J: Uh-uh.

C: So where were you if your life goes back in one unbroken chain all the way back to Adam? You had to be in Adam, right?

J: Uh-huh.

C: When Adam sinned, what did you do?

J: Sinned.

C: When he died, spiritually, what happened to you?

J: Died.

C: So you were born dead.

J: Uh-huh.

C: If you're born dead, and were born a sinner, you committed sins and you were going to stay eternally dead—separated from God, hell—unless something happens. You were born into this life by physical birth, and if you're spiritually dead, what's the greatest need you have?

J: To be spiritually awakened.

C: To be made alive. And how do you get spiritual life?

J: Be saved.

C: By *birth*—spiritual birth. You have to be born again according to John 3:3. So we're born into this life by physical birth, and in the same manner we're born into Christ's life [*pointing to transition from Adam to Christ in Diagram 6*] by spiritual birth. So then you, too, have eternal life. And you have lived forever in the past! Is that right?

J: Uh-huh.

C: You lived forever in the *past!* Now whose life do you have?

J: Christ's.

C: Christ's life. Is this life always the same?

J: Uh-huh.

C: Does it have a beginning?

J: Uh-uh.

C: Does your eternal life have any beginning?

J: Uh-uh.

C: Right here (the point of entry into Christ's life), you tapped in when you were born; you were born into His life. Once you are in His life, you have entered into an eternal existence with Him with no beginning and no end. So back in the Garden of Eden you were in Adam, right? Okay. In the Garden of Gethsemane, where were you? [*Tracing the Line diagram back to and beyond the Cross*]

J: In Christ?

C: In Christ. When Christ was hanging on the cross, where were you?

J: In Christ.

C: So what happened to you?

J: I was crucified with Him.

C: And when He was buried . . . ?

J: I was buried with Him.

C: When He was raised . . . ?

J: I was raised with Him.

C: Where are you now?

J: In Christ; in heaven?

C: I hear a question mark in that statement. Are you seated up there with Him?

J: Uh-huh.

C: Are you accepted in Him?

J: Uh-huh.

C: Are you perfect?

J: Not in my eyes but in His eyes.

C: Seated at His right hand are you perfect?

J: No.

C: What is real? The way God sees you or the way you *feel?*

J: The way God sees me.

C: Since you're seated at the right hand of God, this means that the old man has been nailed to the cross and you have had a new birth and received a new nature. Is there any reason for you to feel inferior if Christ lives His life in you?

J: Uh-uh.

C: Let's look at a passage in the Word here. What does Romans 6, verse 6, say?

J: "Knowing this, that our old man is crucified with him, that the body of sin might be destroyed, that henceforth we should not serve sin."

C: So what got crucified?

J: The old nature.

C: The old nature, the old man. So the thing that you got from Adam that could do nothing but sin was right back at the cross to be crucified.

J: Uh-huh.

C: So if the old nature is crucified, then who's supposed to do the living?

J: Christ.

C: Okay. Now, who *has* been doing the living?

J: Me.

C: This means that self or flesh has been in control, right? If you're doing the living, you'll continue to feel inferior, won't you? Just suppose that you count or reckon upon your death in Christ and let Jesus do the living. Romans 6:11 states that you should reckon or count yourself to be dead unto sin, but alive unto God. Now—if Christ were actually living His life through your person and were in control of your mind so that you are "bringing into captivity every thought to the obedience of Christ" (2 Corinthians 10:5), do you think you would feel inferior?

J:　Uh-uh.

C:　Are you crucified with Him?

J:　Uh-huh.

C:　How do you know?

J:　Because I've trusted in Him for my salvation and His Word says so.

C:　Would you read Ephesians 2:6?

J:　"He hath raised us up together, and made us sit together in heavenly places in Christ Jesus."

C:　Are you accepted?

J:　Uh-huh.

C:　Since you're in Christ, you're in Him at the right hand of God, right? Is Christ in you?

J:　Uh-huh.

C:　Colossians 1:27 says it this way: "Christ *in you,* the hope of glory" [*italics added*]. Your total commitment allows the Holy Spirit to deal with the flesh such that you can reckon yourself to be crucified or dead unto sin and let Christ actually do all the living through you. The day you were saved, were you crucified too?

J:　Uh-huh.

C:　Did you ever know it?

J:　Uh-uh.

C:　You didn't realize that you were there. Do you remember that song "Were You There When They Crucified My Lord?"

J:　Uh-huh.

C:　Well, you *were.* You were not only there, you were *in* Him. You don't have to go on *trying* to live a Christian life, *trying* to please your father, *trying* to please the Lord. Have you already pleased the Lord when you died with the Lord? Read Ephesians 1:6.

J: "To the praise of the glory of his grace, wherein he hath made us accepted in the beloved."

C: Are you *accepted?*

J: Uh-huh.

C: Are you *acceptable?*

J: Uh-huh.

C: Do you have to do anything to be acceptable?

J: No.

C: Look at Hebrews 3:19. Can you read that?

J: "So we see that they could not enter in because of unbelief."

C: So they couldn't enter in to possess their possessions in the land because of unbelief. Now read verse 10, chapter 4.

J: "For he that is entered into his rest, he also hath ceased from his own works, as God did from his."

C: When you've entered into your rest, you've ceased from *your* works. Although you were saved by grace, you've been working for acceptance, haven't you?

J: [*Nods yes*]

C: God says you're not only acceptable, but you can cease from your own works and enter into *His* rest. You can claim by faith the fact that you died in Christ, were buried, raised, and seated at His right hand, and thank God for saving you from yourself. You haven't been doing the best job of it, have you? Now here is the choice you have to make: Do you want to go on trying to live your own life for Him, or let Him live His life through you? If you continue to try to live your life *for* Him, you'll probably mess it up worse than you have already, won't you?

J: Uh-huh.

C: You can't be good enough for God to accept you. He already has. Unless you get your life changed, you can't make it with your dad no matter what you say or do. God says you can cease from your own works and quit trying to do it yourself. You must realize that you are totally *accepted* and totally *acceptable in Christ,* just the way you are. Right now, do you have the righteousness of Christ?

J: No.

C: How did you lose it? Read Second Corinthians 5:21 for me, will you?

J: "For He hath made him to be sin for us, who knew no sin; that *we might be made the righteousness of God in him*" [*italics added*].

C: Do you have His righteousness? Are you holy? It's a hard thing to say that, isn't it? How does God see you?

J: Accepted.

C: Accepted; righteous.

J: Uh-huh.

C: And holy in Christ. We don't have any holiness or righteousness of our own. But God sees you as being in Christ. You're in Christ at the right hand of God. Is there any sin in heaven?

J: Uh-uh.

C: And you're there! So you must be *righteous;* in fact, you are totally acceptable to God in Christ. Do you think you are so dissatisfied with that self-life that you'd like to put an end to its control and just claim by faith that what God says is already true—that since you have died in Christ, you don't have to *try* to live? You can give up on *you!* When you give up *trying* and start *trusting,* it is as though God says, "I've been trying to get you to do that since you were saved!"

God says you died with Christ. The day you were saved, you died two thousand years before and were raised and seated at the right hand of God. Since you were, you can let or reckon Christ to be your life and let Him do the living. Ephesians 1:19, 20 says that all the power that God used to raise the Lord Jesus Christ from the dead is available *in you. There* is power for performance! Galatians 2:20 says, "I am [have been] crucified with Christ: nevertheless I live; yet not *I*, but Christ liveth in me . . ." [*italics added*]. And that's what He wants to do—do the living *in you*. You don't *have* to keep living for Him. Now, do you think you'd like to claim this by faith today? Here is my life, Lord; I don't want to hassle You anymore. I'm tired of trying to live for You, trying to work and do all these things, and trying to prove myself to my dad, or You, or anybody else. The Lord Jesus Christ has already done the atoning; He's done the proving, and now I'm willing to claim my death—that I died with Christ when I was born again. I'm ready to claim by faith the fact that I'm seated at Your right hand and thank You for saving me from *myself* and all the ways I've blown it and actually allow Christ to live in and through me.

Would I be convincing you or persuading you against your will to claim by faith what God says that you are in Him? Do you want to?

J: Uh-huh.

C: [*Bowing head*] Father, thank You for bringing my sister Judy here. I thank You for her sincerity and honesty in wanting to know—to possess—all that she is in Christ. Thank You for her. We trust, now that she has seen her acceptance in Christ, that You might make that acceptance so real, as she accepts it by faith, that she can be free from these things of the past and let You live in glorious victory within her and give her the abundant life. [*Raises head*] Now, Judy, do you want to pray in your own words? [*Extends both hands to her across desk*]

J: [*Extending her hands to clasp his*] Father, thank You for this time; and, Lord, I just pray that I'll learn to accept the facts, Lord, that I learned today, and I see it in a new light that I've never seen it in before. Lord, I thank You for this; and, Lord, I just realize now that I'm accepted in You; and, Lord, I just pray that You'll help me to accept myself as being accepted in You, for there's nothing I have to do to prove to anyone, now. Lord, I thank You for what I've learned today; and I just pray that You'll continue to bring these facts back to my mind. In Your name. Amen.

C: Praise the Lord!

(It is advisable to briefly review Romans 6:6, 11, 13 at this point to anchor the decision of faith to the Word which serves to de-emphasize feelings and emphasize objective Truth.)

Upon returning for the next interview about two weeks later, Judy reported that the Holy Spirit had used a message on love by her pastor to illuminate the truths she had claimed by faith in the interview. She was in victory, with many of the symptoms reduced or gone, and had new insight into the Word of God. The counselor took her to the Word to confirm that which she had claimed by faith as well as to get her better acquainted with it. The third interview consisted primarily of grounding her in the use of her *will* in continuing to appropriate by faith her walk in the Spirit. Just before she left for college a few days later, her mother called and said that Judy must see the counselor. A downer was well in progress, and she was shown how to regain victory by a faith appropriation of her position in Christ. Upon returning from a quarter of college, she reported some defeat but more victory and having shared with some friends at college the identification truths.

She was encouraged to continue study of her position in Christ in Romans 6, 7, and 8 as well as in Galatians, Ephesians, Philippians, and Colossians.

She reported that her father is now able to show her love and that it is a whole new learning experience to be able to accept his love and to communicate this acceptance to him. The counselor has had interviews with the secondborn with good results, and she is now grappling with appropriation of her resources in Christ. The father has reviewed this transcript and confirms the changes in Judy and his relationship with her.

It is just a matter of time until the parents and the two older daughters are able to communicate effectively and to demonstrate their love for each other in a manner previously impossible. Once this is securely established in the individuals and in the family relationships, it is anticipated that they will soon be able to communicate the Christ-life to their friends, both saved and unsaved. Both parents have told the counselor in their home of others who are in dire need of the understanding they have gained.

Reading List

Demonism

Bubeck, Mark I. *The Adversary: The Christian Versus Demon Activity.* Moody Press, Chicago.

Unger, Merrill. *Demons in the World Today.* Tyndale House Publishers, Wheaton, Illinois.

Devotional

Chambers, Oswald. *My Utmost for His Highest.* Dodd, Mead & Company, New York.

Cowman, Mrs. Charles E. *Streams in the Desert.* Zondervan Publishing House, Grand Rapids.

Murray, Andrew. *God's Best Secrets.* Zondervan Publishing House, Grand Rapids.

Family

Christenson, Larry. *The Christian Family.* Bethany Fellowship, Minneapolis.

Dobson, James. *Dare to Discipline.* Tyndale House Publishers, Wheaton, Illinois.

LaHaye, Tim and Beverly. *The Act of Marriage.* Zondervan Publishing House, Grand Rapids.

Narramore, Bruce. *Help! I'm a Parent.* Zondervan Publishing House, Grand Rapids.

Tournier, Paul. *To Understand Each Other.* John Knox Press, Atlanta.

Finances

Bowman, George M. *How to Succeed With Your Money.* Moody Press, Chicago.

Fooshee, George, Jr. *You Can Be Financially Free.* Fleming H. Revell Company, Old Tappan, New Jersey.

Prayer

MacDonald, Hope. *Discovering How to Pray.* Zondervan Publishing House, Grand Rapids.

Murray, Andrew. *The Prayer Life.* Moody Press, Chicago.

Unknown Christian. *The Kneeling Christian.* Zondervan Publishing House, Grand Rapids.

Spiritual Growth

Austin-Sparks, T. Austin. *What Is Man?* Ministry of Life, Cloverdale, Indiana.

Christenson, Larry. *The Renewed Mind.* Bethany Fellowship, Minneapolis.

Epp, Theodore. *The Other Comforter.* Back to the Bible Broadcast, Lincoln, Nebraska.

Harrison, Norman B. *New Testament Living.* His International Service, Minneapolis.

Huegel, F. J. *Bone of His Bone.* Zondervan Publishing House, Grand Rapids.

Hunter, John. *Faith That Works.* Christian Literature Crusade, Fort Washington, Pennsylvania.

———— *Living the Christ-filled Life.* Zondervan Publishing House, Grand Rapids.

Kazee, Buell H. *Faith Is the Victory.* Wm. B. Eeerdmans Publishing Co., Grand Rapids.

LaHaye, Tim. *How to Win Over Depression.* Zondervan Publishing House, Grand Rapids.

Matthews, Victor. *Growth in Grace.* Zondervan Publishing House.

Maxwell, L. E. *Born Crucified.* Moody Press, Chicago.

McConkey, James. *The Threefold Secret of the Holy Spirit.* Back to the Bible Broadcast, Lincoln, Nebraska.

Meyer, F. B. *The Christ-Life for Your Life.* Moody Press, Chicago.

Murray, Andrew, *Abide in Christ.* Christian Literature Crusade, Fort Washington, Pennsylvania.

———— *New Life.* Bethany Fellowship, Minneapolis.

———— *The Prayer Life.* Moody Press, Chicago.

———— *The True Vine.* Moody Press.

———— *Absolute Surrender.* Moody Press.

———— *Waiting on God.* Moody Press.

Nee, Watchman. *Not I, But Christ*. Christian Fellowship Publishers, Manassas, Virginia.

—— *Normal Christian Life*. Christian Literature Crusade, Fort Washington, Pennsylvania.

—— *Sit, Walk, Stand*. Christian Literature Crusade.

—— *Changed Into His Likeness*. Christian Literature Crusade.

Newell, William R. *Romans, Verse by Verse*. Moody Press, Chicago.

Paxson, Ruth. *Rivers of Living Water*. Moody Press.

—— *Life on the Highest Plane*. Moody Press.

Pierson, A.T. *In Christ Jesus*. Moody Press.

Redpath, Alan. *Victorious Christian Living*. Fleming H. Revell Company, Old Tappan, New Jersey.

Smith, Hannah Whitall. *The Christian's Secret of a Happy Life*. Fleming H. Revell Company.

—— *The God of All Comfort*. Moody Press, Chicago.

Solomon, Charles. *Handbook to Happiness*. Tyndale House Publishers, Wheaton, Illinois.

—— *The Ins and Out of Rejection*. Heritage House, Denver.

Stanford, Miles. *Principles of Spiritual Growth*. Back to the Bible Broadcast, Lincoln, Nebraska.

—— *The Green Letters*. Zondervan Publishing House, Grand Rapids.